Materials & Methods for SOCIOLOGY RESEARCH

Library Edition

By James Gruber, Judith Pryor, and Patricia Berge

The library works

A Division Of Neal-Schuman Publishers, Inc.

Published by The Libraryworks
A Division of Neal-Schuman Publishers, Inc.
64 University Place, New York, N.Y. 10003
Copyright © 1980 by Neal-Schuman Publishers, Inc.

Printed and bound in the United States of America.

Library of Congress Cataloging in Publication Data

Gruber, James.
   Materials & methods for sociology reserach.

   (Bibliographic instruction series)
   1. Sociology–Methodology–Handbooks, manuals, etc.
2. Sociological research — Handbooks, manuals, etc.
I. Pryor, Judith, joint author. II. Berge, Patricia, joint
author. III. Title. IV. Series.
   HM24.G77   301'.07'2   79-14814
   ISBN 0-918212-13-8
   ISBN 0-918212-12-X pbk.

Contents

Editorial Board

Preface

Materials & Methods for Sociology Research is the third publication of the "Materials & Methods" bibliographic instruction series developed by Carla Stoffle, Assistant Chancellor for Educational Services at the University of Wisconsin, Parkside, and Henry F. Dobyns, Visiting Professor of Anthropology, University of Florida at Gainesville. Basic to the series is the discipline-oriented workbook, developed and tested in the classroom by librarians and teaching faculty. Intended to guide students through the maze of information sources encountered during their studies, the workbooks are based on the principle that the more students know about the materials and methods required for effective information gathering in their subject discipline, the more productive they will become.

This library edition of *Materials & Methods for Sociology Research* is comprised of the workbook and an instructor's manual. The workbook introduces students to — and requires them to use — a wide variety of reference tools. Chapter by chapter, guides, subject dictionaries, encyclopedias, biographical sources, indexes, abstracts, bibliographies, periodicals, and government documents are explored. The instructor's manual offers suggestions to librarians and teachers; explains the features of the workbook; provides grading, assignment, an scheduling instructions; and includes individualized fill-ins and answers for the problems and questions found in the workbook.

Both the instructor's manual and the workbook are available separately, designed for course adoption. This one-volume, hard cover edition has been published to serve as a reference tool in and of itself, as well as a text for staff training in bibliographic instruction.

Materials & Methods
for
Sociology Research
Instructor's Manual

Table of Contents

Preface

Materials & Methods for Sociology Research is designed to familiarize sociology students with the basic types of information sources available in the discipline, to introduce important examples of each type, and to prepare students to use those information sources efficiently and effectively. The workbook consists of brief textual discussions of individual types of sources and assignments requiring students to use important examples of each type. Instruction and immediate practical application are thus blended to maximize student learning.

The workbook is modeled on the lab manual as used in many science courses. This format was selected after examination of, and experimentation with, several alternative methods for teaching library research skills. There are several advantages in teaching these skills in this manner: (1) the content is broken down into small units that can be mastered easily; (2) the exercises immediately reinforce the textural and class presentation of information; (3) the students actively participate in the learning process; (4) students receive immediate feedback about their progress; (5) student confusion or failure to master the skills can be easily and immediately detected; (6) additional instruction can be provided for those who need it while those who do not can proceed at their own pace; and (7) the number of students that can be taught simultaneously can vary significantly, and almost any course setting, from a separate course to a module within a course, can be used.

As well as introducing principal types of information sources, and principal examples of each type, the workbook is designed to provide students an opportunity to use the sources in a systematic way. It discusses research strategies and the mechanics of the research process, and requires, in the last assignment, that students undertake a research project utilizing the previously learned sources and skills.

The development of the workbook was funded in part by a Teaching Improvement Grant from the University of Wisconsin System, and is the product of three years of experimentation by librarians and a sociologist at the University of Wisconsin-Parkside. During the first year, the instructors relied upon lectures to familiarize students with categories of information sources based on those discussed in Carl White's *Sources of Information in the Social Sciences* (Chicago: American Library Association, 1973), Thelma Freides' *Literature and Bibliography of the Social Sciences* (New York: Wiley, 1973), and *Social Science Research Handbook* by Raymond G. McInnis and James W. Scott (New York: Barnes and Noble, 1974). In subsequent years, the categories were refined and the lectures were distilled to form these brief chapters with clearly stated objectives and assignments that require students to use the sources annotated in each chapter.

This Instructor's Manual is divided into eight sections. Section One describes the organization and scope of the Workbook, and identifies its objectives. A description of how best to use the Workbook is provided in Section Two, as well as suggestions for its use in settings other than a three credit course. Specific suggestions regarding instructional procedures, the role of the library staff, and sources used are given in Section Three. An itemized checklist comprises Section Four, identifying nine tasks for the instructor to accomplish. Section Five provides sample instructions to guide the faculty member in preparing instructions to the students for the course. A Checklist of Titles Used, in Section Six, enables the instructor to determine whether the library owns the exact editions of titles used for the assignments. And Sections Seven and Eight are included to save the instructor the time consuming chore of creating and testing individual question sets for use with the workbook.

1
Arrangement and Scope
of the Workbook

The specific objectives of the workbook are to teach students:

1) to identify and use specialized sociological reference sources such as guides, subject dictionaries and encyclopedias, biographical sources, indexes, abstracts, and bibliographies;
2) to locate articles and book reviews in sociological journals;
3) to locate and use newspaper articles in research;
4) to locate and use government publications in research;
5) to evaluate the quality of books by using reviews and other criteria discussed in the workbook;
6) to utilize specific research techniques and search strategies for efficient and effective information gathering; and
7) to cite periodicals, books, and documents according to standard bibliographic form.

The workbook is organized into twelve chapters. Each of the first eleven describes the purposes and utility of one category or type of publication. Examples of each type are annotated. The sources used as examples were selected after a review of guides and sociological bibliographies and on the basis of three criteria: they are all in the English language; they are generally available in medium sized college libraries; they are important examples of the types of sources most useful to sociology majors.

The assignments accompanying each chapter insure that students immediately use the sources and techniques discussed. The questions pose specific study or research problems. Since needless frustration can only hinder learning, there are no "trick," or even very difficult, questions. Each question is phrased in a manner that reiterates points made in the text about the general utility of a type of source and/or the special utility of an individual source.

To introduce students to sources that list reference works, the first chapter focuses on guides to the literature. Chapters Two through Four introduce content reference sources: handbooks, yearbooks, subject dictionaries, and encyclopedias. Chapters Five and Six introduce the principal types of findings aids: indexes, abstracts, and bibliographies.

The focus of the workbook then shifts away from reference materials. In Chapters Seven, general periodicals and newspapers are examined; in Chapter Eight scholarly journals are discussed; in Chapter Nine methods for evaluating the quality of monographs are suggested. Chapters Ten and Eleven focus on government publications, and upon the finding aids available for their efficient use. Chapter Twelve, the last chapter, consists of a discussion of strategies, mechanics, and methods for efficient library research. Students are asked to define a research topic and prepare a bibliography, using as many of the types of sources introduced in the previous chapters as may be appropriate. This summary assignment requires students to review the preceding chapters. It reiterates for them the interrelated utility of the sources discussed in the separate chapters, and demonstrates to them that in a relatively short time they have learned much about the library's resources and how to use them.

On the average, the workbook absorbs roughly 20-25 hours of out-of-class student time. Individual assignment sheet questions should require no more than 20 minutes, although at first they often require more time since students are generally unfamiliar with reference sources.

2
Use of the Workbook

At the University of Wisconsin-Parkside, the workbook is used as an integral part of a three credit sociology methods course. A librarian teaches the four weeks of the course that focus on library research. The class meets in the library. For class purposes, the library becomes a lab where students must locate and use specified publications to complete their assignments. With the exception of periodicals, which must be kept on reserve for the duration to insure their availability, all of the noncirculating publications used in the assignments are left in their normal place in the library. A comfortable familiarity with the reference area is one of the benefits students derive from using the workbook.

At the introductory meeting, the librarian describes the workbook, its purposes and organization, and the procedures that will be followed. Students who have had no previous library instruction are given a tour of the library and are offered supplementary instruction on the card catalogue. Attendance at subsequent class sessions is optional, although most students do attend. At these sessions the librarian provides additional information about the uses and organization of the types of sources discussed in the assigned chapters and answers questions. Before each class period, the students should have read the appropriate chapters and completed the assignments.

To discourage self-defeating forms of student cooperation, the assignments are individualized. Although every student reads the same question, each is for a different item of information. Each question contains a "fill-in" space or spaces designated by the black underlines. Twenty different sets of fill-ins — containing the specific information requests — are provided in Section Seven. Copies of these fill-in sheets are distributed to the students along with instruction sheets (see Section Five). Each student is asked to transfer the "fill-in" information from the sheet to the workbook. When more than twenty students are enrolled in the course, some sets of fill-ins are given to more than one student.

Assignments may be turned in during the class period or may be placed in a specially marked container next to the reference desk in the library. Assignments are corrected daily by the librarian (using the answer sheets in Section Eight), and are placed on designated shelves in the reference area so that students may pick them up and continue their work without delay. Credit is not given for a chapter until all questions are answered correctly. When students must make a correction, they are instructed to ask the reference librarian on duty for help. The reference librarian thus becomes a tutor, providing the student with whatever instruction is necessary to correct the mistake. And, the student becomes familiar not only with the library's resources, but also with its personnel and their willingness to assist students.

The workbook is graded on a pass-fail basis. No credit is given until all the questions in all the assignments are correctly answered. In addition, the bibliography assigned in Chapter Twelve must be completed to the satisfaction of both the librarian and the faculty member in charge of the course. The specific criteria used in grading the bibliography at the University of Wisconsin-Parkside are included with the instructions handed out to the students when they begin the manual (see Section Five). The sociology faculty member in charge of the course gives students who do not complete the work satisfactorily a grade of incomplete for the course, or a failing grade for that portion of the course.

The workbook can effectively be used in settings other than a three credit methods course. These include: other sociology courses with a research focus; one or two credit courses devoted exclusively to sociology bibliography; independent or guided study courses; noncredit study or continuing education programs; and graduate library science courses. In credit sociology courses, faculty may wish to employ team teaching techniques similar to those used at the University of Wisconsin-Parkside.

Faculty who wish to use the workbook but who do not want to devote a significant amount of class time to it or who wish to have students use the manual independently should contact the library staff for support services and suggestions. Arrangements might be made for students to rely upon specified library staff members for tutorial assistance while they are completing the assignments. It may be possible to have the library staff distribute the fill-in sheets and grade the assignments as well.

For noncredit uses of the workbook in school or public libraries, the instructor or librarian may want to provide the students with the answer sheets so that they can correct their own assignments. In these cases, the instruction sheets, assignment fill- in sheets, and answer sheets can be distributed to the students all in one packet.

3
Specific Suggestions

INSTRUCTIONAL PROCEDURES

The value of library research skills is not always readily apparent to students. The instructor may want to introduce the workbook with a discussion of student research needs and problems, and a discussion of the purposes of the workbook.

The time students should be given to complete the workbook depends on the course format. A semester is too long a period. Given too much time, students tend to fall behind, and then do several chapters in a rushed, short period of time. On the other hand, if given too little time students do not carefully read and digest the information. The results are usually careless mistakes in the assignments. The workbook should not be assigned during the last four weeks of any quarter or semester.

Because all students use the same titles to complete the assignments, there is a possibility that some students will have to wait while others use particular sources. This is especially likely if the assignments are worked on during the class period. If students do the assignments during the class period, frustration over having to wait for the sources can be minimized by having them work on the questions in differing orders or, whenever possible, by having multiple copies of an assigned source.

At the start, students may have a tendency to try to complete the assignments without carefully reading both the text and the questions. The instructor should emphasize that the assignments can be done correctly and efficiently only after a careful reading of the material. The instructor should warn students about problems they may encounter if they do not examine the reference sources carefully. In some cases, the too casual student will find a partially correct answer but not the best answer for a question.

The organization of some sources, such as indexes and abstracts, is fairly complex. It is advisable to supplement the workbook and class discussion of those sources with transparencies and/or handouts demonstrating their use.

The fill-in sheets in Section Seven should be photocopied for distribution to the students. If more than twenty students are enrolled in the course, some fill-in sheets will have to be given to more than one student. To forestall, if not prevent, students with the same sets identifying each other, the instructor may wish to modify the book numbers on the fill-in sheets so that they may be easily identified for grading purposes only.

Assignments should be corrected and returned to the students as quickly as possible. Immediate feedback is a requirement for optimal effectiveness of the workbook as an instructional source. A system that allows students to hand in assignments as they complete them and pick up corrected exercises from a shelf in the library rather than during the class period has the advantage of providing immediate feedback, and further implements the library as laboratory concept.

Although the workbook can be graded on any basis, a pass/fail system is suggested since it provides a more relaxed atmosphere for the students and poses fewer problems of administration than other grading systems.

The assignments need not be corrected by a faculty member or professional librarian; however, those assignments which contain errors should be seen by the instructor or the librarian. In some cases, although the student may have used the source correctly, a careless mistake writing down the answer could have been made. The instructor must decide how rigidly students will be held to supplying answers exactly as they appear on the answer sheets in Section Eight. There can be a fair amount of flexibility as to what will be accepted. The determinative test should be whether the student has demonstrated an understanding of how to use the source. Many questions ask the students to identify the page on which they found the information requested. This is generally asked to aid the instructor or reference librarian in determining why a student erred in located the substantive information called for in the question. If the student provides the information correctly but not the page number, the instructor may decide that no useful educational purpose is served by having the student recheck the page number.

ROLE OF THE LIBRARY STAFF

The general reference staff can be very helpful to students if staff members are informed about plans for using the workbook, the schedule for the assignments, the nature of the questions, the exact location of the sources, and any special instructions given the students.

For students unfamiliar with the library, the staff may provide some initial general instruction about such things as the physical location of materials, the arrangement of the card catalogue and periodicals, and any special symbols or location devices used in the library.

Publications should be left on the shelves if they are part of a noncirculating collection, such as the reference collection, in order to provide the students with a realistic research environment. The work of the library staff will be kept to a minimum if the materials do not have to be handled by the reserve staff every time students use them. However, for publications in the general stacks and other publications whose use involves long delays before they are returned to the shelves (periodicals for example), the reserve collection may be the only viable location.

To minimize student frustration, it is essential that publications, other than those in the reserve collection, be on the shelves in their proper location. Circulation and reference staffs should be provided with a list of the titles and classification numbers of these publications, and asked to watch for them to insure their return as quickly as possible after use. It may be of help to tag or mark publications with a colored tape to indicate to staff that these are materials that should be reshelved immediately. If they are accidently misshelved, they are likely to be noticed more quickly if they are marked.

SOURCES

The library's holdings should be checked using the alphabetical list of annotated sources in Section Six. For books and indexes, the edition and/or volumes used in questions are identified. Journals are cited by the year, volume, and/or issue number. If a publication annotated in this workbook is not owned by the library and a decision is made not to purchase it, an appropriate publication, annotation, and question can be substituted.

If large numbers of students (more than 20-25 at a time) will be using the workbook, the instructor may want to have the library provide additional copies of some publications. Large groups can be accomodated without multiple copies, but this may require additional preparation and planning.

New editions of reference works may cause some problems for instructors using the fill-ins and answers supplied in Sections Seven and Eight. In some cases, only the page number of the answer will change. In other cases, yearbooks for example, the information requested may be unavailable or changed in the new editions. Therefore, if a new edition of a source is used, the questions will have to be checked and correct answers substituted on the answer sheets in Section Eight. Old editions may be kept on the reference shelves for several years to reduce the frequency of changes in questions and answers required by changes in editions. If this procedure is used, students should be warned to use the appropriate editions.

When a publication for which there is an assignment cannot be located, the instructor may opt for any one of several alternative procedures. Students can be asked to use the publication in another library; a substitute question can be prepared; in cases where questions are taken from several volumes of a source and only one volume is missing, students can be provided with different fill-ins; or, the question can always be dropped. Multiple copies of one-volume works would, of course, eliminate the problem. Students could also be told that there will be no excuse accepted for not completing an assignment in an effort to obviate the possibility that publications will disappear while the course is in progress.

4
Instructor's Checklist

1. Check the sources annotated in the workbook against the holdings of your library. Be sure your library owns the issues or editions used in the questions. Section Six contains an alphabetical list of the sources, with the appropriate issues or editions specified.

2. For distribution to the students, prepare a list of the publications for which there are questions and place the call numbers for the publications on the list. You may want to arrange the publications in alphabetical order by title or list them by chapter. A sample list is contained in Section Five.

3. Prepare instruction packets for the students. Section Five contains a sample of instructions. Be sure to include:
   a. a question fill-in sheet, with instructions to write the sheet number and the fill-ins on the assignment pages in the workbook;
   b. a schedule for the assignments;
   c. information about the grading system; and
   d. special instructions regarding such things as the turning in and returning of assignments, and publications which have been placed in the reserve collection or in other special locations in the library.

4. Make necessary arrangements regarding the publications which must be placed on reserve, moved, or in some way marked.

5. Notify the reference, circulation, and cataloging staffs in writing about the instruction program and any special procedures they should follow while the workbook is in use. Provide them with copies of the instructions given to the students.

6. Provide a copy of the workbook to the reference staff so that staff members may examine it before they are approached for help by students working on their assignments.

7. Prepare a student evaluation form for feedback about the usefulness of this instructional program and suggestions on ways in which procedures and materials can be made more effective.

8. Prepare a list of criteria that will be used in evaluating the student bibliographies and research "logs." These criteria should be communicated to the students in the instruction sheets (see the sample in Section Five).

9. Prepare a grade sheet to record completed assignments for each student. For each assignment, record the date of completion. Be sure that the number for the set of question fill-ins and answers assigned to each student is recorded next to the student's name. This will allow you to be sure that students do not turn in answers to fill-ins not their own on a particular assignment and will enable you to replace correctly and easily their fill-in sheet should they lose it.

5
Samples of Materials for Distribution to Students During the First Class Period

The sample set of instructions on the following pages includes a schedule for completing the workbook based on a semester course meeting twice a week, as well as details on the assignments and how they can be graded. A sample list of sources has also been provided with call numbers. It is arranged by chapter to facilitate student use of the workbook.

6
Checklist of Titles Used in Assignments

This list is provided to facilitate checking the holdings of your library against the titles used in the assignments. Please pay particular attention to the date of the edition for each title. The answers provided in Section Eight are taken from the editions specified in this checklist.

American Journal of Sociology. Chicago: University of Chicago Pr., 1895—.
—vol. 76, nos. 4, 5,6
—vol. 77, no. 4
—vol. 78, nos. 1, 2, 3
—vol. 79, no. 2
—vol. 80, nos. 1, 2, 3, 4, 6
—vol. 81, nos. 5, 6
—vol. 82, nos. 1, 3, 4, 5, 6
American Sociological Review. Washington, D. C.: American Sociological Association, 1936—.
—vol. 37, nos. 1, 2, 3, 4, 5, 6
—vol. 38, nos. 1, 2, 3, 4, 5, 6
American Statistics Index. Washington, D. C: Congressional Information Service, 1973—.
—1975
—1976
—1977
Annual Review of Sociology. Palo Alto, Calif.: Annual Reviews, 1975—.
—1975

—1976
—1977
—1978
Bibliographic Index. New York: Wilson, 1937—.
—1973
—1974
—1975
—1976
—1977
U. S. Bureau of the Census. *Bureau of the Census Catalog.* Washington, D. C.: Government Printing Office, 1790—.
—1974
—1975
—1976
CIS/Index to Publications of the United States Congress. Washington, D. C.: James B. Adler, 1970—.
—1974
—1975
—1976

Continued on p. 13

SAMPLE

INSTRUCTIONS

Assignments

The assignments in this workbook are individualized. No two students in the class are asked to look up the same item of information. Attached are the fill-in portions of the questions. This set is unique to you. Please write your name and the number of this set of fill-ins on the cover, title page, and on each assignment page of your workbook. Then, for each assignment, write the fill-ins on the underlined spaces in the questions. Staple the fill-in sheet to the back cover of your workbook. You may want to refer to it later to insure that all information was copied correctly.

Schedule

The following is a schedule of due dates for all assignments. You may work ahead, but please avoid falling behind. Assignments may be turned in during the class period, or you may place them anytime in the bin marked "Deposit Workbooks Here," next to the Information Desk. The corrected sheets will be placed on the "Pick Up Workbooks Here" shelves next to the Information Desk. They will be arranged alphabetically by your last name.

September 15	Chapters 1 - 3
September 20	Chapters 4 - 5
September 22	Chapters 6 - 7
September 27	Chapters 8 - 9
September 29	Chapters 10-11
October 4	Chapter 12 & Bibliography

SAMPLE

Grading

The workbook will be administered on a complete/incomplete basis. Each assignment will be checked and errors will be identified. Credit will not be given for an assignment until all questions have been answered correctly.

The final assignment, the preparation of a bibliography, and a journal recording the steps taken and sources used in the research, must be completed to the satisfaction of both the instructor and the librarian.

The bibliography will be checked against the following criteria:

1. The appropriateness of the titles cited as sources of information for a research paper in an advanced sociology course. Factors which will be considered include the authors' reputations, the copyright dates, the publishers' reputations, the reputation of the journals, etc.

2. The appropriateness of the titles cited as sources for the specific topic being researched.

3. The number of titles cited. Although the suitable number of titles will vary from subject to subject, a bibliography of less than fifteen titles raises, in most cases, the question of completeness.

4. The correctness of the bibliographic citation forms.

The journal should reflect the use of a reasonable variety of reference sources in the research. There must be a sound reason given in the journal for consulting each reference source.

SAMPLE

Special Information

Please read carefully the "Note to the Student" section in your workbook. If you follow the suggested procedures, your work will be much less burdensome. Additionally, keep the following in mind:

1. Only those sources which are annotated have questions in the assignment section of each chapter.

2. Most publications will be found according to the classification numbers provided on the attached list.

3. Journals and books normally available in the circulating collection will be kept at the Reserve Desk.

SAMPLE

LIST OF SOURCES WITH LIBRARY OF CONGRESS CALL NUMBERS

Chapter 1 - Guides to the Literature

Guide to Reference Books
REF. Z 1035.1 S43 1976

Sources of Information in the Social Sciences
REV. Z 7161 W49 1973

Chapter 2 - Handbooks

County and City Data Book
REF. HA 202 A36 1977

Handbook of Social Psychology
REF. HM 251 L486

Historical Statistics of the United States: Colonial Times to 1970
REF. HA 202 A385 1975

Chapter 3 - Yearbooks

Annual Review of Sociology
HM 1 A763 (On Reserve)

Demographic Yearbook
REF. HA 17 D45 1975

Statistical Yearbook
REF. HA 12.5 U63 1977

Uniform Crime Reports for the United States
REF. HV 6787 A3 1977

Chapter 4 - Subject Dictionaries and Encyclopedias

International Encyclopedia of the Social Sciences
REF. H 40 A215

Dictionary of Sociology
REF. HM 17 M56 1968b

Chapter 5 – Abstracts and Indexes

Criminal Justice Abstracts
IND. HV 6001 C7

Population Index
IND. HB 848 P6

Social Science Citation Index
IND. Z 7161 S65

Sociological Abstracts
IND. HM 1 S67

Chapter 6 – Bibliographies

Bibliographic Index
IND. Z 1002 B595

International Bibliography of Sociology
REF. Z 7161 I594

Subject Catalog: A Cumulative List of Works Represented by Library
   of Congress Printed Cards
CAT. Z 881 A1 C325

Chapter 7 – General Periodicals and Newspapers

New York Times Index
IND. AI 21 N452

NewsBank: Urban Affairs Library
IND. AI 3 N4

Society
PER.

Chapter 8 – Scholarly Journals

American Journal of Sociology
PER.

American Sociological Review
PER.

Journal of Marriage and the Family
PER.

Magazines for Libraries
REF./OFF. Z 6941 K2 1978

Social Forces
PER.

Chapter 9 - Evaluating Book-length Studies

Contemporary Sociology: A Journal of Reviews
PER.

Chapter 10 - United States Government Publications

CIS/Index to Publications of the United States Congress
IND. DF 49 C62

Cumulative Subject Index to the Monthly Catalog of United States
    Government Publications, 1900-1971
IND. Z 1223 Z7B8

Monthly Catalog of the United States Government Publications
IND. Z 1223 A18

Chapter 11 - United States Census Publications

American Statistics Index
IND. Z 7161 A5

Bureau of the Census Catalog
IND. Z 1223 C42

Contemporary Sociology: A Journal of Reviews. Washington, D. C.: American Sociological Association, 1971—.
—vol. 6, nos. 1, 2, 3, 4
—vol. 7, nos, 1, 2, 3

U. S. Bureau of the Census. *County and City Data Book.* Washington, D. C.: Government Printing Office, 1949—.
—1977 edition

New York Times Index. New York: New York Times, 1913—.
—1938
—1967
—1969
—1971
—1975
—1976

NewsBank: Urban Affairs Library. Greenwich, Conn.: 1975—.
—1975 edition

Population Index. Princeton, N. J.: Office of Population Research, Princeton University and Population Association of America, 1935—.
—1974
—1975
—1976

Social Forces. Chapel Hill, N. C.: University of North Carolina Pr., 1922—.
—vol. 49, September 1970, December 1970, March 1971, June 1971
—vol. 50, December 1971, March 1972, June 1972
—vol. 51, September 1972, December 1972, March 1973
—vol. 53, September 1974, December 1974, March 1975, June 1975

Social Sciences Citation Index. Philadelphia Institute for Scientific Information, 1972—.
—1974
—1975

Social Sciences Index. New York: H. W. Wilson, 1974/75—.
—vol. 1, April 1974-March 1975
—vol. 2, April 1975-March 1976
—vol. 3, April 1976-March 1977

Society. (Formerly: *Transaction: Social Science and Modern Society.*) New Brunswick, N. J.: Rutgers—The State University, 1967—.
—vol. 10, nos. 1, 2, 3, 4
—vol. 11, nos. 1, 2, 3, 4, 5, 6
—vol. 12, nos. 1, 2, 3, 4, 5, 6
—vol. 13, nos. 1, 3, 4, 5

Sociological Abstracts. New York: Sociological Abstracts, 1952—.
—1972
—1973
—1974
—1975
—1976
—1977

White, Carl. *Sources of Information in the Social Sciences.* 2nd ed. Chicago: American Library Association, 1973.

United Nations. Statistical Office. *Statistical Yearbook.* New York: 1949—.
—1976 edition

Criminal Justice Abstracts. Hackensack, N. J.: National Council on Crime and Delinquency, 1968—.
—vol. 8, 1976 (*Crime and Delinquency Literature*)
—vol. 9, 1977

Cumulative Subject Index to the Monthly Catalog of United States Government Publications, 1900-1971. Washington, D. C.: Carrollton Pr., 1973.

United Nations. Statistical Office. *Demographic Yearbook.* New York: 1948—.
—1975 edition

Mitchell, G. Duncan. *Dictionary of Sociology.* Chicago: Aldine, 1968.

Sheehy, Eugene P. *Guide to Reference books.* 9th ed. Chicago: American Library Association, 1976.

Lindzey, Gardner and Elliot Aronson, eds. *Handbook of Social Psychology.* 2nd ed. Reading, Mass.: Addison-Wesley, 1968-69—.
—5 vols.

Historical Statistics of the United States: Colonial Times to 1970. Washington, D. C.: Government, Printing Office, 1975.
—2 vols.

International Bibliography of Sociology. London: Tavistock, 1951—.
—vol. 20, 1970
—vol. 22, 1972
—vol. 23, 1973
—vol. 24, 1974
—vol. 25, 1975

International Encyclopedia of the Social Sciences. New York: Macmillan, 1968—.
—17 vols.

Katz, William. *Magazines for Libraries.* 3rd ed. New York: Bowker, 1978—.

U. S. Superintendent of Documents. *Monthly Catalog of United States Government Publications.* Washington, D. C.: Government Printing Office, 1885—.
—1964
—1965
—1966
—1968
—1969
—1970
—1971

U. S. Library of Congress. *Subject Catalog: A Cumulative List of Works Represented by Library of Congress Printed Cards.* Washington, D. C.: 1950—.
—1965-1969
—1970-1974

U. S. Federal Bureau of Investigation. *Uniform Crime Reports for the United States.* Washington, D. C.: Government Printing Office, 1930—.
—1977 edition.

7
Assignment Fill-In Sheets

Copies of the assignment sheets should be distributed to the students with instructions to: (1) write the fill-in sheet number (which appears on the upper right hand corner) on each assignment page of their workbooks; (2) write the appropriate information in the underlined spaces provided for each question; and (3) staple the fill-in sheets to the back cover of the workbook for future reference. The "Q" indicates question numbers in the assignments.

MATERIALS & METHODS FOR
SOCIOLOGY RESEARCH

Fill-ins by Book

Book No. __1__

CHAPTER ONE
Q.2.   an introduction to forestry course
Q.3.   guides to the literature

CHAPTER TWO
Q.2.   cognitive theories
Q.3.   north central
       1860
Q.4.   a. Autauga, Alabama
       b. Bronx, N.Y.

CHAPTER THREE
Q.2.   Canada
Q.3.   Angola
Q.4.   robbery using firearms
       a. over 250,000
       b. 25,000–50,000
Q.5.   age differentiation

CHAPTER FOUR
Q.2.   cooperation
Q.3.   anomie

CHAPTER FIVE
Q.3.   alcohol and youth
       April 1957–March 1976
Q.4.   Algeria
       1976
Q.5.   advertising
       1973
Q.6.   child abuse
       1977
Q.7.   S. M. Dornbusch
       Social Forces, vol. 33, 1955, p. 316
       1975

CHAPTER SIX
Q.2.   alcoholism
       1977
Q.3.   political parties
       vol. 25, 1975

Q.4.   acculturation
       1970–1974

CHAPTER SEVEN
Q.2.   a. busing
          Birmingham, Alabama
          San Francisco, California
Q.3.   abortion
       1976
Q.4.   "A Life Record of an Immigrant"
       November/December 1975

CHAPTER EIGHT
Q.2.   vol. 80, no. 1, July 1974
       a. "A Model for Occupational Careers"
Q.3.   vol. 37, no. 1, 1972
       a. Joel H. Levine
Q.4.   vol. 49, September 1970
       a. *Racial Policies and Practices of Real Estate Brokers*
          by Rose Helper
Q.5.   *American Journal of Sociology*

CHAPTER NINE
Q.2.   *Sociological Model for Identifying Alcoholics:*
          Experimental Design
       Y. C. Kim
       vol. 1, April 1974 to March 1975
Q.3.   *Why Survive?: Being Old in America*
       Robert N. Butler
       vol. 7, no. 3, May 1978

CHAPTER TEN
Q.2.   alcoholism
       1975
Q.3.   anti-poverty campaign

CHAPTER ELEVEN
Q.2.   kidnapping
       1976
Q.3.   household characteristics
       1974

MATERIALS & METHODS FOR
SOCIOLOGY RESEARCH

Fill-ins by Book

Book No.   2

CHAPTER ONE

Q.2. a comparative religion course
Q.3. reviews of the literature and research

CHAPTER TWO

Q.2. field theory
Q.3. northeast
      1800
Q.4. a. Baldwin, Alabama
      b. Erie, N.Y.

CHAPTER THREE

Q.2. Costa Rica
Q.3. Burma
Q.4. robbery using firearms
      a. 50,000–100,000
      b. under 10,000
Q.5. political socialization

CHAPTER FOUR

Q.2. neighborhoods
Q.3. animism

CHAPTER FIVE

Q.3. aged–family relationships
      April 1975-March 1976
Q.4. Ghana
      1976
Q.5. childrearing
      1973
Q.6. halfway houses
      1977
Q.7. A. S. Dreyer
      Human Relations, vol. 7, 1954, p. 175
      1975

CHAPTER SIX

Q.2. rape
      1977
Q.3. political elite
      vol. 25, 1975
Q.4. drugs
      1970-1974

CHAPTER SEVEN

Q.2. a. busing
      Kentucky
      Wisconsin
Q.3. housing discrimination in Alabama
      1976
Q.4. "Police Vigilantes"
      March/April 1976

CHAPTER EIGHT

Q.2. vol. 80, no. 2, September 1974
      a. "Analysis of Ratio Variables: Opportunities
      and Pitfalls"
Q.3. vol. 37, no. 1, 1972
      a. David Britt and Omer R. Galle
Q.4. vol. 49, September 1970
      a. *Middle Class Families: Social and
      Geographical Mobility* by Colin Bell
Q.5. *American Sociological Review*

CHAPTER NINE

Q.2. *Measuring Religious Dimensions*
      M. B. King and R. A. Hunt
      vol. 1, April 1974 to March 1975
Q.3. *Jewish South Africans: A Sociological
      View of the Johannesburg Community*
      Allie A. Dubb
      vol. 7, no. 3, May 1978

CHAPTER TEN

Q.2. anti-Semitism
      1975
Q.3. anti-poverty program

CHAPTER ELEVEN

Q.2. family abandonment
      1976
Q.3. birth expectations
      1974

MATERIALS & METHODS FOR
SOCIOLOGY RESEARCH

Fill-ins by Book

Book No. __3__

CHAPTER ONE

Q.2.   an introduction to linguistics course
Q.3.   comprehensive abstracting services

CHAPTER TWO

Q.2.   role theory
Q.3.   northeast
       1810
Q.4.   a. Barbour, Alabama
       b. Kings, N.Y.

CHAPTER THREE

Q.2.   Cuba
Q.3.   Kenya
Q.4.   robbery using firearms
       a. 100,000-250,000
       b. 10,000-25,000
Q.5.   theories in collective behavior

CHAPTER FOUR

Q.2.   cross pressure
Q.3.   bureaucracy

CHAPTER FIVE

Q.3.   marriage in Turkey
       April 1975-March 1976
Q.4.   Nigeria
       1976
Q.5.   deviant behavior
       1973
Q.6.   rape
       1977
Q.7.   F. F. Furstenberg
       American Sociological Review, vol. 31,
         1966, p. 326
       1975

CHAPTER SIX

Q.2.   drugs and youth
       1977
Q.3.   political leadership
       vol. 25, 1975
Q.4.   white collar crimes
       1970-1974

CHAPTER SEVEN

Q.2.   a. busing
          Minneapolis, Minnesota
          Jefferson Co., Alabama
Q.3.   gambling
       1976
Q.4.   "Urban Disamenities"
       May/June 1976

CHAPTER EIGHT

Q.2.   vol. 80, no. 3, November 1974
       a. "Religious Orthodoxy and Minority Prejudice:
          Causal Relationship or Reflection of Localistic
          World View?"
Q.3.   vol. 37, no. 2, 1972
       a. William L. Parish, Jr. and Moshe Schwartz
Q.4.   vol. 49, December 1970
       a. *General Theory of Population* by Alfred Sauvy
Q.5.   *British Journal of Sociology*

CHAPTER NINE

Q.2.   *Social Groups in Polish Society*
       D. Lane and G. Kolankiewicz
       vol. 1, April 1974 to March 1975
Q.3.   *Murder in Space City: A Cultural Analysis of
         Houston Homicide Patterns*
       Henry P. Lundsgaarde
       vol. 7, no. 3, May 1978

CHAPTER TEN

Q.2.   child welfare
       1975
Q.3.   metropolitan poverty areas

CHAPTER ELEVEN

Q.2.   child day care
       1976
Q.3.   college plans of high school seniors
       1976

MATERIALS & METHODS FOR
SOCIOLOGY RESEARCH

Fill-ins by Book

Book No. __4__

CHAPTER ONE

Q.2. a world literature course
Q.3. specialized abstracting services

CHAPTER TWO

Q.2. organizations
Q.3. northeast
      1820
Q.4. a. Bibb, Alabama
      b. Monroe, N.Y.

CHAPTER THREE

Q.2. Dominican Republic
Q.3. Nigeria
Q.4. strongarmed robbery
      a. over 250,000
      b. 25,000-50,000
Q.5. patterns of family interaction

CHAPTER FOUR

Q.2. adolescence
Q.3. category

CHAPTER FIVE

Q.3. prisons
      April 1975-March 1976
Q.4. Canada
      1976
Q.5. interviews
      1972
Q.6. school violence
      1977
Q.7. D. Glaser
      American Sociological Review, vol. 19,
        1954, p. 335
      1975

CHAPTER SIX

Q.2. sexual deviation
      1977
Q.3. political socialization
      vol. 25, 1975

Q.4. mentally ill children
      1970-1974

CHAPTER SEVEN

Q.2. a. aid to families with dependent children
         Wisconsin
         Oklahoma
Q.3. families
      1976
Q.4. "Political Alienation"
      July/August 1976

CHAPTER EIGHT

Q.2. vol. 80, no. 4, January 1975
      a. "Women and the Fear of Success:
         A Problem in Replication"
Q.3. vol. 37, no. 2, 1972
      a. Samuel Leinhardt
Q.4. vol. 49, March 1971
      a. *International Community Power Structures*
         by Delbert C. Miller
Q.5. *International Journal of Comparative Sociology*

CHAPTER NINE

Q.2. *Essence of Social Research: A Copernican Revolution*
      C. W. Lachenmeyer
      vol. 1, April 1974 to March 1975
Q.3. *Nine Mayan Women: A Village Faces Change*
      Mary Elmendorf
      vol. 7, no. 2, March 1978

CHAPTER TEN

Q.2. civil rights
      1975
Q.3. business and poverty

CHAPTER ELEVEN

Q.2. discrimination in employment by age
      1976
Q.3. mobility of the population
      1974

MATERIALS & METHODS FOR
SOCIOLOGY RESEARCH

Fill-ins by Book

Book No. __5__

CHAPTER ONE

Q.2.   an introduction to astronomy course
Q.3.   current comprehensive bibliographies

CHAPTER TWO

Q.2.   psychology of religion
Q.3.   northeast
       1840
Q.4.   a. Blount, Alabama
       b. Nassau, N.Y.

CHAPTER THREE

Q.2.   El Salvador
Q.3.   South Africa
Q.4.   strongarmed robbery
       a. 50,000-100,000
       b. under 10,000
Q.5.   macrosociology

CHAPTER FOUR

Q.2.   Anglo-American society
Q.3.   sociometry

CHAPTER FIVE

Q.3.   public housing in Colombia
       April 1975-March 1976
Q.4.   Egypt
       1976
Q.5.   mental health
       1972
Q.6.   wife-beating
       1977
Q.7.   R. L. Helmreich
       Journal of Experimental and Social Psychology,
          vol. 4, 1968, p. 153
       1975

CHAPTER SIX

Q.2.   juvenile delinquency
       1977
Q.3.   political elite
       vol. 23, 1973
Q.4.   homosexuality
       1970-1974

CHAPTER SEVEN

Q.2.   a. police-community relations
          Arkansas
          California
Q.3.   alcoholism
       1976
Q.4.   "Class, Family, and Housing"
       November/December 1974

CHAPTER EIGHT

Q.2.   vol. 80, no. 6, May 1975
       a. "Toward a Subcultural Theory of Urbanism"
Q.3.   vol. 37, no. 3, 1972
       a. Lawrence E. Hazelrigg and Joseph Lopreato
Q.4.   vol. 49, June 1971
       a. *Christian Converts and Social Protest in Meiji Japan*
          by Irwin Scheiner
Q.5.   *Jewish Journal of Sociology*

CHAPTER NINE

Q.2.   *Socioeconomic Background and Educational*
          Performance
       R. M. Hauser
       vol. 1, April 1974 to March 1975
Q.3.   *Dual-Career Families Re-examined: New*
          Integrations of Work and Family
       Rhona Rapoport and Robert N. Rapoport
       vol. 7, no. 2, March 1978

CHAPTER TEN

Q.2.   abortion
       1975
Q.3.   children and poverty

CHAPTER ELEVEN

Q.2.   refugees
       1976
Q.3.   living arrangements
       1974

MATERIALS & METHODS FOR
SOCIOLOGY RESEARCH

Fill-ins by Book

Book No. ___6___

CHAPTER ONE

Q.2.   a basic chemistry course
Q.3.   current specialized bibliographies

CHAPTER TWO

Q.2.   experimentation
Q.3.   northeast
       1850
Q.4.   a. Bullock, Alabama
       b. New York, N.Y.

CHAPTER THREE

Q.2.   Honduras
Q.3.   Sudan
Q.4.   strongarmed robbery
       a. 100,000-250,000
       b. 10,000-25,000
Q.5.   health care delivery systems

CHAPTER FOUR

Q.2.   assimilation
Q.3.   class-consciousness

CHAPTER FIVE

Q.3.   birth control in India
       April 1974-March 1975
Q.4.   Brazil
       1976
Q.5.   stereotyping
       1972
Q.6.   capital punishment
       1977
Q.7.   R. Herberle
       Social Movements, 1951, p. 269
       1975

CHAPTER SIX

Q.2.   gambling
       1976
Q.3.   political leadership
       vol. 23, 1973

Q.4.   prison discipline
       1970-1974

CHAPTER SEVEN

Q.2.   a. police-community relations
          Florida
          New Jersey
Q.3.   divorce in Australia
       1976
Q.4.   "Ethnic Genocide"
       January/February 1975

CHAPTER EIGHT

Q.2.   vol. 81, no. 5, March 1976
       a. "The Real Self: From Institution to Impulse"
Q.3.   vol. 37, no. 4, 1972
       a. Lee Freese
Q.4.   vol. 50, March 1972
       a. *The American Family: A Sociological Interpretation*
          by Bert N. Adams
Q.5.   *Journal of Marriage and the Family*

CHAPTER NINE

Q.2.   *Making It In Prison, the Square, the Cool, and the Life*
       E. Heffernan
       vol. 1, April 1974 to March 1975
Q.3.   *Sociological Research: Philosophy and Methods*
       Henry L. Manheim
       vol. 7, no. 2, March 1978

CHAPTER TEN

Q.2.   disabled American veterans
       1975
Q.3.   the church and anti-poverty programs

CHAPTER ELEVEN

Q.2.   drug abuse and treatment
       1976
Q.3.   family characteristics
       1974

MATERIALS & METHODS FOR
SOCIOLOGY RESEARCH

Fill-ins by Book

Book No. __7__

CHAPTER ONE
Q.2. an introductory geology course
Q.3. retrospective bibliographies

CHAPTER TWO
Q.2. observational methods
Q.3. north central
      1800
Q.4. a. Butler, Alabama
      b. Onondaga, N.Y.

CHAPTER THREE
Q.2. Uruguay
Q.3. Bahamas
Q.4. aggravated assault with a firearm
      a. over 250,000
      b. 25,000-50,000
Q.5. the structure of organizations

CHAPTER FOUR
Q.2. Caribbean society
Q.3. collective conscience

CHAPTER FIVE
Q.3. children, their civil rights
      April 1974-March 1975
Q.4. Australia
      1976
Q.5. family planning
      1974
Q.6. effect of imprisonment
      1977
Q.7. M. W. Hicks
      Journal of Marriage and the Family,
          vol. 32, 1970
      1975

CHAPTER SIX
Q.2. drugs and youth in the United States
      1976
Q.3. political culture
      vol. 23, 1973
Q.4. juvenile detention homes
      1970-1974

CHAPTER SEVEN
Q.2. a. police-community relations
      Washington, D.C.
      California
Q.3. drug addiction
      1967
Q.4. "Secret Intelligence Agencies and Congress"
      March/April 1975

CHAPTER EIGHT
Q.2. vol. 81, no. 6, May 1976
      a. "Network Sampling: Some First Steps"
Q.3. vol. 37, no. 5, 1972
      a. Darwin L. Thomas, David D. Franks, and
         James M. Calonico
Q.4. vol. 50, March 1972
      a. *Opportunity and the Family* by
         John H. Scanzoni
Q.5. *Journal of Social Issues*

CHAPTER NINE
Q.2. *Motherless Families*
      V. George and P. Wilding
      vol. 1, April 1974 to March 1975
Q.3. *Women in the Organization*
      Harold H. Frank
      vol. 7, no. 1, January 1978

CHAPTER TEN
Q.2. discrimination in employment
      1975
Q.3. education and poverty

CHAPTER ELEVEN
Q.2. public welfare programs
      1976
Q.3. marital status
      1974

MATERIALS & METHODS FOR
SOCIOLOGY RESEARCH

Fill-ins by Book

Book No. ___8___

CHAPTER ONE
Q.2. an introduction to mineralogy course
Q.3. directories

CHAPTER TWO
Q.2. interviewing
Q.3. north central
      1810
Q.4. a. Calhoun, Alabama
      b. Queens, N.Y.

CHAPTER THREE
Q.2. Cyprus
Q.3. Cuba
Q.4. aggravated assault with a firearm
      a. 50,000-100,000
      b. under 10,000
Q.5. sociological study of deviant behavior

CHAPTER FOUR
Q.2. civil disobedience
Q.3. conurbation

CHAPTER FIVE
Q.3. cities and towns—population distribution
      April 1974-March 1975
Q.4. Pakistan
      1976
Q.5. peasantry
      1974
Q.6. vandalism
      1977
Q.7. V. C. Nahirny
      American Journal of Sociology, vol. 67,
      1962, p. 397
      1975

CHAPTER SIX
Q.2. sexual deviation
      1976
Q.3. political parties
      vol. 23, 1973

Q.4. divorce
      1970-1974

CHAPTER SEVEN
Q.2. a. women police
      California
      Iowa
Q.3. alcoholism
      1969
Q.4. "West Point: Cadets, Codes and Careers"
      May/June 1975

CHAPTER EIGHT
Q.2. vol. 82, no. 1, July 1976
      a. "On the Sociology of National Development:
      Theories and Issues"
Q.3. vol. 37, no. 5, 1972
      a. Edna Bonacich
Q.4. vol. 50, June 1972
      a. *The Urban Mosaic* by Duncan Timms
Q.5. *Pacific Sociological Review*

CHAPTER NINE
Q.2. *Urban Anthropology: Cross-cultural Studies of
      Urbanization*
      A. Southall
      vol. 2, April 1975 to March 1976
Q.3. *Experimenter Effects in Behavioral Research*
      Robert Rosenthal
      vol. 7, no. 1, January 1978

CHAPTER TEN
Q.2. discrimination in housing
      1975
Q.3. characteristics of the employed poor

CHAPTER ELEVEN
Q.2. illegitimacy
      1975
Q.3. educational attainment in the U.S.
      1974

MATERIALS & METHODS FOR
SOCIOLOGY RESEARCH

Fill-ins by Book

Book No. 9

CHAPTER ONE
Q.2.   a basic music theory course
Q.3.   dictionaries

CHAPTER TWO
Q.2.   content analysis
Q.3.   north central
       1820
Q.4.   a. Chambers, Alabama
       b. Suffolk, N.Y.

CHAPTER THREE
Q.2.   Israel
Q.3.   Greenland
Q.4.   aggravated assault with a firearm
       a. 100,000-250,000
       b. 10,000-25,000
Q.5.   adult socialization

CHAPTER FOUR
Q.2.   criminology
Q.3.   criminology

CHAPTER FIVE
Q.3.   crime and criminals in Florida
       April 1974-March 1975
Q.4.   Egypt
       1975
Q.5.   guilt
       1974
Q.6.   marijuana laws reform
       1977
Q.7.   M. Northway
       Sociometry, vol. 10, 1947, p. 186
       1975

CHAPTER SIX
Q.2.   rape
       1976
Q.3.   political elite
       vol. 22, 1972
Q.4.   children of divorced parents
       1970-1974

CHAPTER SEVEN
Q.2.   a. women police
       Maine
       Nebraska
Q.3.   crime and criminals in California
       1969
Q.4.   "Simulating Society"
       July/August 1975

CHAPTER EIGHT
Q.2.   vol. 82, no. 3, November 1976
       a. "Structural Change in Social Processes"
Q.3.   vol. 37, no. 6, 1972
       a. Charles E. Hurst
Q.4.   vol. 50, December 1971
       a. *People and Information* edited by
       Harold Pepinsky
Q.5.   *Small Group Behavior*

CHAPTER NINE
Q.2.   *Social Construction of Communities*
       G. D. Suttles
       vol. 2, April 1975 to March 1976
Q.3.   *The Plantation School*
       Anthony Gerald Albanese
       vol. 7, no. 1, January 1978

CHAPTER TEN
Q.2.   educational facilities
       1976
Q.3.   extent of poverty in the U.S.

CHAPTER ELEVEN
Q.2.   discrimination in employment by age
       1975
Q.3.   family by type
       1976

MATERIALS & METHODS FOR
SOCIOLOGY RESEARCH

Fill-ins by Book

Book No. 10

CHAPTER ONE

Q.2. an introduction to French literature course
Q.3. encyclopedias

CHAPTER TWO

Q.2. cross-cultural research
Q.3. north central
1830
Q.4. a. Cherokee, Alabama
b. Westchester, N.Y.

CHAPTER THREE

Q.2. Japan
Q.3. Honduras
Q.4. aggravated assault with hands, fists, and feet
a. over 250,000
b. 25,000-50,000
Q.5. race/ethnic relations

CHAPTER FOUR

Q.2. deviant behavior
Q.3. cross-cousin

CHAPTER FIVE

Q.3. divorce
April 1974-March 1975
Q.4. Ghana
1975
Q.5. ceremonies
1975
Q.6. prison strikes
1977
Q.7. S. Nosow
Social Forces, vol. 35, 1956, p. 25
1975

CHAPTER SIX

Q.2. conjugal violence
1976
Q.3. political leadership
vol. 22, 1972
Q.4. father—separated children
1970-1974

CHAPTER SEVEN

Q.2. a. women police
Maryland
Wisconsin
Q.3. robberies and thefts in Egypt
1969
Q.4. "Television: Mass Communication and Elite Controls"
September/October 1975

CHAPTER EIGHT

Q.2. vol. 82, no. 4, January 1977
a. "Problematics in Stratum Consistency and
Stratum Formation: An Australian Example"
Q.3. vol. 37, no. 6, 1972
a. Larry L. Bumpass and James A. Sweet
Q.4. vol. 50, December 1971
a. *Sociology and Social Work: Perspectives and
Problems* by Brian J. Heraud
Q.5. *Rural Sociology*

CHAPTER NINE

Q.2. *American Public Opinion: Its Origins, Content,
and Impact*
R. S. Erikson and N. R. Luttbeg
vol. 2, April 1975 to March 1976
Q.3. *Democracy and Organisation in Chinese
Industrial Enterprise, 1948-1953*
William Brugger
vol. 6, no. 1, January 1977

CHAPTER TEN

Q.2. energy conservation
1976
Q.3. poverty and food

CHAPTER ELEVEN

Q.2. school dropouts
1975
Q.3. household and family characteristics
1975

MATERIALS & METHODS FOR
SOCIOLOGY RESEARCH

Fill-ins by Book

Book No. __11__

CHAPTER ONE

Q.2. an introduction to the biological sciences course
Q.3. handbooks

CHAPTER TWO

Q.2. social motivation
Q.3. north central
      1840
Q.4. a. Chilton, Alabama
      b. Bristol, Mass.

CHAPTER THREE

Q.2. Jordan
Q.3. Jamaica
Q.4. aggravated assault with hands, fists, and feet
      a. 50,000-100,000
      b. under 10,000
Q.5. international migration

CHAPTER FOUR

Q.2. economy and society
Q.3. demography

CHAPTER FIVE

Q.3. social structure
      April 1976-March 1977
Q.4. Nigeria
      1975
Q.5. stress
      1975
Q.6. employee theft
      1976
Q.7. I. Nye
      American Sociological Review, vol. 16,
          1951, p. 341
      1975

CHAPTER SIX

Q.2. alcoholism
      1975
Q.3. political socialization
      vol. 22, 1972
Q.4. rehabilitation of juvenile delinquents
      1970-1974

CHAPTER SEVEN

Q.2. a. women police
         New Jersey
         Washington
Q.3. prisons and prisoners in Maine
      1969
Q.4. "Reform School Families"
      November/December 1973

CHAPTER EIGHT

Q.2. vol. 82, no. 5, March 1977
      a. "Ending the Vietnam War: Components of Change
         in Senate Voting on Vietnam War Bills"
Q.3. vol. 38, no. 1, 1973
      a. James S. Coleman
Q.4. vol. 50, June 1972
      a. *The Spiral of Conflict: Berkeley, 1964*
         by Max Heirich
Q.5. *Social Forces*

CHAPTER NINE

Q.2. *Economic Foundations of Political Power*
      R. Bartlett
      vol. 2, April 1975 to March 1976
Q.3. *Immigrants and Politics*
      Paul R. Wilson
      vol. 6, no. 1, January 1977

CHAPTER TEN

Q.2. Mexican Americans
      1976
Q.3. growing up poor

CHAPTER ELEVEN

Q.2. minority groups
      1975
Q.3. fertility expectations of American women
      1975

MATERIALS & METHODS FOR
SOCIOLOGY RESEARCH

Fill-ins by Book

Book No. __12__

CHAPTER ONE

Q.2. a Spanish literature course
Q.3. yearbooks

CHAPTER TWO

Q.2. attitudes and attitude change
Q.3. north central
      1850
Q.4. a. Choctow, Alabama
      b. Essex, Mass.

CHAPTER THREE

Q.2. Belgium
Q.3. Guatemala
Q.4. aggravated assault with hands, fists, and feet
      a. 100,000-250,000
      b. 10,000-25,000
Q.5. sample surveys

CHAPTER FOUR

Q.2. elites
Q.3. eidos

CHAPTER FIVE

Q.3. empathy
      April 1976-March 1977
Q.4. Tanzania
      1975
Q.5. stereotypes
      1975
Q.6. rural crime
      1976
Q.7. E. Suzuki
      Principles of Rural Sociology, 1940
      1975

CHAPTER SIX

Q.2. drug abuse in the United States
      1975
Q.3. political doctrine
      vol. 22, 1972
Q.4. police services for juveniles
      1970-1974

CHAPTER SEVEN

Q.2. a. prostitution
      Alabama
      Idaho
Q.3. prisons and prisoners in Michigan
      1969
Q.4. "The Dual Welfare System"
      January/February 1974

CHAPTER EIGHT

Q.2. vol. 82, no. 6, May 1977
      a. "Identity Loss, Family, and Social Change"
Q.3. vol. 38, no. 1, 1973
      a. Andrew Hopkins
Q.4. vol. 53, September 1974
      a. *Soviet and American Society: A Comparison*
      by Paul Hollander
Q.5. *Social Problems*

CHAPTER NINE

Q.2. *Ethnic Diversity in Catholic America*
      H. J. Abramson
      vol. 2, April 1975 to March 1976
Q.3. *Pursuing the American Dream: White Ethnics and
      the New Populism*
      Richard Krickus
      vol. 6, no. 1, January 1977

CHAPTER TEN

Q.2. migrant and seasonal workers
      1976
Q.3. housing conditions in poverty areas

CHAPTER ELEVEN

Q.2. Oriental Americans
      1975
Q.3. family by type
      1975

MATERIALS & METHODS FOR
SOCIOLOGY RESEARCH

Fill-ins by Book

Book No. _13_

CHAPTER ONE

Q.2. a basic physics course
Q.3. original sources

CHAPTER TWO

Q.2. socialization
Q.3. south
1800
Q.4. a. Clarke, Alabama
b. Hampden, Mass.

CHAPTER THREE

Q.2. Austria
Q.3. Mexico
Q.4. burglary by forcible entry
a. over 250,000
b. 25,000-50,000
Q.5. precapitalist social structures

CHAPTER FOUR

Q.2. fashion
Q.3. essentialism

CHAPTER FIVE

Q.3. groups (sociology)
April 1976-March 1977
Q.4. India
1975
Q.5. powerlessness
1975
Q.6. organized crime
1976
Q.7. E. M. Suval
Social Forces, vol. 43, 1965, p. 536
1975

CHAPTER SIX

Q.2. gangs
1975
Q.3. political elite
vol. 24, 1974
Q.4. police services for juveniles
1965-1969

CHAPTER SEVEN

Q.2. a. prostitution
Arizona
Maryland
Q.3. gambling
1938
Q.4. "Ethnic Resentment"
March/April 1974

CHAPTER EIGHT

Q.2. vol. 76, no. 4, January 1971
a. "Class and Marriage in Africa and Eurasia"
Q.3. vol. 38, no. 2, 1973
a. Edward O. Laumann and Franz Urban Pappi
Q.4. vol. 53, September 1974
a. *Mountain Families in Transition* by Harry K.
Schwarzweller, James S. Brown, and J. J. Mangalam
Q.5. *Social Research*

CHAPTER NINE

Q.2. *Interpersonal Behavior in Small Groups*
R. J. Ofshe
vol. 2, April 1975 to March 1976
Q.3. *Blue Collar Stratification: Autoworkers
in Four Countries*
William H. Form
vol. 6, no. 2, March 1977

CHAPTER TEN

Q.2. poverty
1976
Q.3. law and poverty

CHAPTER ELEVEN

Q.2. venereal disease
1975
Q.3. households by type
1975

MATERIALS & METHODS FOR
SOCIOLOGY RESEARCH

Fill-ins by Book

Book No. 14

CHAPTER ONE

Q.2. an aeronautical engineering basics course
Q.3. statistical sources

CHAPTER TWO

Q.2. psycholinguistics
Q.3. south
      1810
Q.4. a. Clay, Alabama
      b. Middlesex, Mass.

CHAPTER THREE

Q.2. Bulgaria
Q.3. Nepal
Q.4. burglary by forcible entry
      a. 50,000-100,000
      b. under 10,000
Q.5. use of mathematical models in sociological research

CHAPTER FOUR

Q.2. friendship
Q.3. ethnocentrism

CHAPTER FIVE

Q.3. ideology
      April 1976-March 1977
Q.4. Israel
      1975
Q.5. civil rights
      1976
Q.6. prostitutes
      1976
Q.7. H. Nelli
      American Journal of Sociology, vol. 74,
          1969, p. 383
      1974

CHAPTER SIX

Q.2. rape
      1975
Q.3. political conflict
      vol. 24, 1974
Q.4. rehabilitation of juvenile delinquents
      1965-1969

CHAPTER SEVEN

Q.2. a. prostitution
         Delaware
         Indiana
Q.3. crime and criminals in Alaska
      1975
Q.4. "Massport vs. Community"
      May/June 1974

CHAPTER EIGHT

Q.2. vol. 76, no. 5, March 1971
      a. "On Transcending the Absurd: An Inquiry in the
         Sociology of Meaning"
Q.3. vol. 38, no. 3, 1973
      a. Claude S. Fischer
Q.4. vol. 53, December 1974
      a. *The Unexpected Community* by Arlie Russell
         Hochschild
Q.5. *Sociological Inquiry*

CHAPTER NINE

Q.2. *View From the Boys: A Sociology of Downtown
         Adolescents*
      H. J. Parker
      vol. 2, April 1975 to March 1976
Q.3. *Queuing and Waiting: Studies in the Social
         Organization of Access and Delay*
      Barry Schwartz
      vol. 6, no. 2, March 1977

CHAPTER TEN

Q.2. rape
      1976
Q.3. low-income life styles

CHAPTER ELEVEN

Q.2. discrimination in employment
      1975
Q.3. college plans of high school seniors
      1975

MATERIALS & METHODS FOR
SOCIOLOGY RESEARCH

Fill-ins by Book

Book No. __15__

CHAPTER ONE

Q.2. an introduction architecture course
Q.3. a guide to the literature

CHAPTER TWO

Q.2. esthetics
Q.3. south
1820
Q.4. a. Cleburne, Alabama
b. Norfolk, Mass.

CHAPTER THREE

Q.2. Czechoslovakia
Q.3. Brazil
Q.4. burglary by forcible entry
a. 100,000-250,000
b. 10,000-25,000
Q.5. attitudes and behavior

CHAPTER FOUR

Q.2. literacy
Q.3. ethology

CHAPTER FIVE

Q.3. social surveys
April 1976-March 1977
Q.4. United Kingdom; Great Britain
1975
Q.5. environment
1976
Q.6. counseling of rape victims
1976
Q.7. M. Patchen
Human Relations, vol. 11, 1958, p. 303
1974

CHAPTER SIX

Q.2. juvenile delinquency
1975
Q.3. political leadership
vol. 24, 1974
Q.4. father—separated children
1965-1969

CHAPTER SEVEN

Q.2. a. prostitution
New Jersey
South Carolina
Q.3. drug addiction, abuse, and traffic in Cuba
1975
Q.4. "Political Misuses of Crime Rates"
July/August 1974

CHAPTER EIGHT

Q.2. vol. 76, no. 6, May 1971
a. "Race, Maternal Authority, and Adolescent
Aspiration"
Q.3. vol. 38, no. 3, 1973
a. Robert M. Hauser and David L. Featherman
Q.4. vol. 53, March 1975
a. *Control: The Basis of Social Order*
by Paul Sites
Q.5. *Sociological Quarterly*

CHAPTER NINE

Q.2. *Circle of Madness: On Being Insane and
Institutionalized in America*
R. Perrucci
vol. 3, April 1976 to March 1977
Q.3. *The Prison: Policy and Practice*
Gordon Hawkins
vol. 6, no. 2, March 1977

CHAPTER TEN

Q.2. sex discrimination
1976
Q.3. poverty in rural areas of the U.S.

CHAPTER ELEVEN

Q.2. discrimination in employment
1977
Q.3. mobility of the population of the U.S.
1970-1975
1975

MATERIALS & METHODS FOR
SOCIOLOGY RESEARCH

Fill-ins by Book

Book No. 16

CHAPTER ONE

Q.2. an introduction to chemical engineering course
Q.3. reviews of the literature and research

CHAPTER TWO

Q.2. leadership
Q.3. south
      1830
Q.4. a. Coffee, Alabama
      b. Suffolk, Mass.

CHAPTER THREE

Q.2. Denmark
Q.3. Uruguay
Q.4. burglary by unlawful entry
      a. over 250,000
      b. 25,000-50,000
Q.5. the sociology of law

CHAPTER FOUR

Q.2. life tables
Q.3. euphoria

CHAPTER FIVE

Q.3. alcohol and women
      April 1976-March 1977
Q.4. Australia
      1975
Q.5. radicalism
      1976
Q.6. citizen patrols
      1977
Q.7. J. D. Photiades
      American Journal of Sociology, vol. 67,
          1962, p. 666
      1974

CHAPTER SIX

Q.2. drug abuse in the United States
      1974
Q.3. political attitudes
      vol. 24, 1974
Q.4. children of migrant laborers
      1965-1969

CHAPTER SEVEN

Q.2. a. pornography and obscenity
      Arizona
      Massachusetts
Q.3. drug addiction, abuse, and traffic in Jamaica
          (West Indies)
      1975
Q.4. "Rightist Regimes and American Interests"
      September/October 1974

CHAPTER EIGHT

Q.2. vol. 77, no. 4, January 1972
      a. "Objectivity as Strategic Ritual: An Examination
         of Newsmen's Notions of Objectivity"
Q.3. vol. 38, no. 4, 1973
      a. Whitney Pope
Q.4. vol. 53, June 1975
      a. *Old Men Drunk and Sober* by Howard M. Bahr
         and Theodore Caplow
Q.5. *Sociological Review*

CHAPTER NINE

Q.2. *Anarchy, State, and Utopia*
      R. Nozick
      vol. 3, April 1976 to March 1977
Q.3. *Theoretical Approaches to Deviance: An Evaluation*
      Charles E. Frazier
      vol. 6, no. 3, May 1977

CHAPTER TEN

Q.2. child welfare
      1976
Q.3. sickness and poverty

CHAPTER ELEVEN

Q.2. drug abuse and treatment
      1977
Q.3. fertility of American women
      1976

MATERIALS & METHODS FOR
SOCIOLOGY RESEARCH

Fill-ins by Book

Book No. _17_

CHAPTER ONE

Q.2. a costume design course
Q.3. comprehensive abstracting services

CHAPTER TWO

Q.2. cultural psychology
Q.3. south
        1840
Q.4. a. Colbert, Alabama
        b. Worcester, Mass.

CHAPTER THREE

Q.2. Hungary
Q.3. Ecuador
Q.4. burglary by unlawful entry
        a. 50,000-100,000
        b. under 10,000
Q.5. laboratory experimentation in sociological research

CHAPTER FOUR

Q.2. magic
Q.3. folkways

CHAPTER FIVE

Q.3. employment in Puerto Rico
        April 1976-March 1977
Q.4. Egypt
        1974
Q.5. suicide
        1976
Q.6. ex-offender groups
        1977
Q.7. G. Psathas
        Sociometry, vol. 23, 1960, p. 177
        1974

CHAPTER SIX

Q.2. sexual deviation
        1974
Q.3. political socialization
        vol. 20, 1970

Q.4. divorce in the United States
        1965-1969

CHAPTER SEVEN

Q.2. a. pornography and obscenity
        Michigan
        New Hampshire
Q.3. prisons and prisoners in Arizona
        1975
Q.4. "Unions vs. Workers"
        November/December 1972

CHAPTER EIGHT

Q.2. vol. 78, no. 1, July 1972
        a. "Insiders and Outsiders: A Chapter in the
        Sociology of Knowledge"
Q.3. vol. 38, no. 4, 1973
        a. Paul Ritterband and Richard Silberstein
Q.4. vol. 51, September 1972
        a. *Sentencing as a Human Process* by John Hogarth
Q.5. *Sociology and Social Research*

CHAPTER NINE

Q.2. *Culture's Influence on Behaviour*
        R. Serpell
        vol. 3, April 1976 to March 1977
Q.3. *Justice, Legal Systems, and Social Structure*
        H. Richard Hartzler
        vol. 6, no. 3, May 1977

CHAPTER TEN

Q.2. civil rights
        1974
Q.3. socioeconomic trends in poverty areas

CHAPTER ELEVEN

Q.2. school dropouts
        1977
Q.3. household and family characteristics
        1976

MATERIALS & METHODS FOR
SOCIOLOGY RESEARCH

Fill-ins by Book

Book No. 18

CHAPTER ONE

Q.2. an introduction to dentistry course
Q.3. specialized abstracting service

CHAPTER TWO

Q.2. national character
Q.3. south
      1850
Q.4. a. Conecuh, Alabama
      b. Fairfield, Conn.

CHAPTER THREE

Q.2. Greece
Q.3. Yemen
Q.4. burglary by unlawful entry
      a. 100,000-250,000
      b. 10,000-25,00
Q.5. religion

CHAPTER FOUR

Q.2. Marxist sociology
Q.3. ideal type

CHAPTER FIVE

Q.3. family size
      April 1976-March 1977
Q.4. Nigeria
      1974
Q.5. liberalism
      1977
Q.6. prison industry
      1977
Q.7. I. L. Reiss
      Transactions, vol. 5, p. 26
      1974

CHAPTER SIX

Q.2. juvenile delinquency
      1974
Q.3. political power in the United States
      vol. 20, 1970

Q.4. juvenile detention homes
      1965-1969

CHAPTER SEVEN

Q.2. a. pornography and obscenity
      Texas
      Washington, D. C.
Q.3. welfare work in Colorado
      1975
Q.4. "Group Dieting Rituals"
      January/February 1973

CHAPTER EIGHT

Q.2. vol. 78, no. 2, September 1972
      a. "The Positive Functions of Poverty"
Q.3. vol. 38, no. 5, 1973
      a. H. W. Smith
Q.4. vol. 51, September 1972
      a. *The Sociology of Accidents* by Lynda P. Malik
Q.5. *Sociometry*

CHAPTER NINE

Q.2. *Interorganization Theory*
      A. R. Negandhi
      vol. 3, April 1976 to March 1977
Q.3. *Army Politics in Cuba, 1898-1958*
      Louis A. Pérez, Jr.
      vol. 6, no. 3, May 1977

CHAPTER TEN

Q.2. defense industries
      1974
Q.3. vocational training for low-income residents
      of public housing

CHAPTER ELEVEN

Q.2. family abandonment
      1977
Q.3. educational attainment in the U.S.
      1976

MATERIALS & METHODS FOR
SOCIOLOGY RESEARCH

Fill-ins by Book

Book No. __19__

CHAPTER ONE

Q.2. an electrical engineering course
Q.3. current comprehensive bibliographies

CHAPTER TWO

Q.2. collective behavior
Q.3. south
      1860
Q.4. a. Coosa, Alabama
      b. Hartford, Conn.

CHAPTER THREE

Q.2. Iceland
Q.3. Afghanistan
Q.4. theft of automobiles
      a. over 250,000
      b. 25,000-50,000
Q.5. mortality trends

CHAPTER FOUR

Q.2. mass society
Q.3. ideology

CHAPTER FIVE

Q.3. aged—institutional care
      April 1976-March 1977
Q.4. Tanzania
      1974
Q.5. Darwinism
      1977
Q.6. white-collar crime
      1977
Q.7. H. H. Ross
      Gerontology, vol. 8, 1968, p. 50
      1974

CHAPTER SIX

Q.2. narcotic addicts
      1974
Q.3. political power in the U.S.S.R.
      vol. 20, 1970
Q.4. homosexuality
      1965-1969

CHAPTER SEVEN

Q.2. a. patriotism
         Alaska
         Georgia
Q.3. divorce, separations, and annulments
      1971
Q.4. "Apartheid Medicine"
      March/April 1973

CHAPTER EIGHT

Q.2. vol. 78, no. 3, November 1972
      a. "Toward the Sociology of Esoteric Culture"
Q.3. vol. 38, no. 5, 1973
      a. Edna Bonacich
Q.4. vol. 51, December 1972
      a. *Interfaith Marriages: Who and Why* by
         Paul H. Besanceney S. J.
Q.5. *Family Process*

CHAPTER NINE

Q.2. *Social Control of Gambling*
      G. E. Moody
      vol. 3, April 1976 to March 1977
Q.3. *The Age of Capital, 1848-1875*
      E. J. Hobsbawm
      vol. 6, no. 4, July 1977

CHAPTER TEN

Q.2. disabled American veterans
      1974
Q.3. women's role in war on poverty

CHAPTER ELEVEN

Q.2. illegitimacy
      1977
Q.3. household by type
      1976

MATERIALS & METHODS FOR
SOCIOLOGY RESEARCH

Fill-ins by Book

Book No. _20_

CHAPTER ONE

Q.2. an electronic data processing course
Q.3. current specialized bibliographies

CHAPTER TWO

Q.2. infrahuman animals
Q.3. south
1870
Q.4. a. Covington, Alabama
b. New Haven, Conn.

CHAPTER THREE

Q.2. Netherlands
Q.3. Indonesia
Q.4. theft of automobiles
a. 50,000-100,000
b. under 10,000
Q.5. the military

CHAPTER FOUR

Q.2. minorities
Q.3. neighborhood

CHAPTER FIVE

Q.3. married women
April 1976-March 1977
Q.4. China
1974
Q.5. obscenity
1977
Q.6. unreported crime
1977
Q.7. T. O. Carlton
Social Work, Vol. 17, 1972, p. 66
1974

CHAPTER SIX

Q.2. alcoholism
1973
Q.3. political parties in Sweden
vol. 20, 1970
Q.4. mentally ill children
1965-1969

CHAPTER SEVEN

Q.2. a. patriotism
Idaho
Rhode Island
Q.3. alcoholism
1967
Q.4. "Consciousness, Power and Drug Effects"
May/June 1973

CHAPTER EIGHT

Q.2. vol. 79, no. 2, September 1973
a. "Howard W. Odum: The Implications of Folk,
Planning, and Regionalism"
Q.3. vol. 38, no. 6, 1973
a. Sandra J. Ball-Rokeach
Q.4. vol. 51, March 1973
a. *Functionaries* by F. William Howton
Q.5. *Jewish Social Studies*

CHAPTER NINE

Q.2. *Origins of the Liberal Welfare Reforms*
J. R. Hay
vol. 3, April 1976 to March 1977
Q.3. *Friends and Lovers*
Robert Brain
vol. 6, no. 4, July 1977

CHAPTER TEN

Q.2. discrimination in housing
1974
Q.3. women in poverty

CHAPTER ELEVEN

Q.2. civil rights
1977
Q.3. world growth rates
1976

8
Answer Sheets

Because the student assignment pages are an integral part of the workbook, the most convenient way to proceed is to have students turn in the entire workbook periodically for the evaluation of assigned work. At any given time, therefore, the instructor is likely to have in hand a number of workbooks with more than one completed assignment to correct. To facilitate grading, the answer sheets are arranged by complete book. No answer has been written for the first question in each chapter because it is possible for students to provide different yet correct answers. Also, it provides the instructor with a means for determining whether each student has an adequate overall understanding of the type of source under discussion.

Although the answers provided on the following pages have been carefully checked and tested, students may interpret the questions differently, or through means not previously used by any other student, uncover a different and yet correct answer. These possibilities should be kept in mind by the instructor while grading the assignments.

MATERIALS & METHODS FOR
SOCIOLOGY RESEARCH

Answers by Book

Book No. __1__

CHAPTER ONE
Q.2. a. *Woods Words: A Comprehensive Dictionary of Loggers Terms*
  b. p. 827
Q.3. a. *The Student Sociologist's Handbook*
  b. p. 260

CHAPTER TWO
Q.2. a. vol. 1, p. 320
  b. Abelson, R. P.
    1961 "Do predispositional factors summate?" American Psychologist 16:377.
Q.3. a. 9,097
  b. p. 22
Q.4. a. 19.7%
  b. 15.5%

CHAPTER THREE
Q.2. a. 2.00 per 1,000 population
  b. p. 428
Q.3. a. 14.7 per 1,000 population
  b. 47.2 per 1,000 population
  c. p. 79
Q.4. a. 234.7
  b. 48.0
  c. p. 157
Q.5. a. Glen H. Elder, Jr. *Age Differentiation and the Life Course.*
  b. P. Ariès
  c. vol. 1, p. 165

CHAPTER FOUR
Q.2. a. *Cooperation Among Animals, with Human Implications*
  b. vol. 3, p. 390
Q.3. a. Emile Durkheim
  b. p. 7

CHAPTER FIVE
Q.3. a. Jessor, R. and S. L. Jessor
    1975 "Adolescent development and the onset of drinking: a longitudinal study." Journal of Studies on Alcohol 36:27-51.
  b. p. 25
Q.4. a. *Research Monograph Series*
  b. p. 457
Q.5. a. John Howard and Spencer F. Tinkham. "A Framework for Understanding Social Criticism of Advertising"
  b. p. 481
Q.6. a. "The Role of the Child in Child Abuse: A Review of the Literature"
  b. p. 86
Q.7. B. B. Khleif. "Professionalization of School Superintendents—Sociocultural Study of an Elite Program"

CHAPTER SIX
Q.2. a. James Haskins. *Teen-age Alcoholism.*
  b. p. 12

Q.3. a. D. S. Gatlin. "Party Identification, Status, and Race in the South: 1952-1972"
  b. p. 170
Q.4. a. Bennett, Lee A.
    1972 Effects of White Contact on the Lower Skagit Indians. Seattle: Washington Archaeological Society.
  b. vol. 1, p. 144

CHAPTER SEVEN
Q.2. a. 71:E6-7; 4:F8
  b. "Pointer Turns Down Extensive Busing Affecting Berry High"
Q.3. a. Draft of proposed 1r to be issued by RC bishops seeking cooperation of all Amers in amending Const to prohibit abortion is being circulated among bishops
  b. January 3, p. 35, column 4
Q.4. a. Helena Znaniecki Lopata
  b. Loyola University

CHAPTER EIGHT
Q.2. a. Aage B. Sorensen
  b. University of Wisconsin-Madison
  c. 1972 meeting of the American Sociological Association, New Orleans, August 28-31
Q.3. a. "The Sphere of Influence"
  b. Berkowitz, Stephen
    1971 The Dynamics of Elite Structure. Ph.D. Dissertation, Brandeis University.
Q.4. a. F. D. Freedman
  b. San Francisco State College
  c. p. 149
Q.5. a. *Social Sciences Citation Index*
  b. p. 811

CHAPTER NINE
Q.2. *Quarterly Journal of Studies on Alcohol,* 35, no. 3B: 1163-4, S '74. M. M. Hyman.
Q.3. a. Erdman Palmore
  b. Duke University
  c. pp. 280-81

CHAPTER TEN
Q.2. a. S201-9.6
  b. p. 641
  c. David P. Taylor, Asst Sec, Manpower and Reserve Aff, AF
Q.3. a. (64) 6117
  b. "Address by Secretary of Commerce Luther H. Hodges Prepared for Delivery Before the 10th Annual Installation of Officers and Awards Banquet of Peninsula Manufacturers Association, Palo Alto, Calif." 1964. 7 p.

CHAPTER ELEVEN
Q.2. a. 6244-1
  b. p. 27
Q.3. a. p. 104
  b. 101 p.

MATERIALS & METHODS FOR
SOCIOLOGY RESEARCH

Answers by Book

Book No. _2_

CHAPTER ONE
Q.2. a. *Dictionary of Comparative Religion*
b. p. 254
Q.3. a. *American Journal of Sociology*
b. p. 261

CHAPTER TWO
Q.2. a. vol. 1, p. 412
b. Adler, D. L. and J. Kounin
1939 "Some factors operating at the moment of resumption of interrupted tasks." Journal of Psychology 7:355-67.
Q.3. a. 2,636
b. p. 22
Q.4. a. 18.2%
b. 7.0%

CHAPTER THREE
Q.2. a. 0.17 per 1,000 population
b. p. 428
Q.3. a. 14.7 per 1,000 population
b. 39.5 per 1,000 population
c. p. 79
Q.4. a. 67.9
b. 18.0
c. pp. 157-58
Q.5. a. Richard G. Niemi and Barbara I. Sobieszek. *Political Socialization.*
b. P. R. Abramson
c. vol. 3, p. 209

CHAPTER FOUR
Q.2. a. *The Hobo: The Sociology of the Homeless Man*
b. vol. 11, p. 124
Q.3. a. Sir E. B. Taylor
b. p. 6

CHAPTER FIVE
Q.3. a. Berkman, B. and H. Rehr
1975 "Elderly patients and their families: factors related to satisfaction with hospital social services." Gerontologist 15:524-28.
b. p. 13
Q.4. a. *Population Growth and Socioeconomic Change in West Africa*
b. p. 229
Q.5. a. Jerry J. Bigner. "Parent Education in Popular Literature: 1950-1970"
b. p. 1123
Q.6. a. *Halfway Houses*
b. p. 295
Q.7. J. B. Rijsman. "Factors in Social Comparison of Performance Influencing Actual Performance"

CHAPTER SIX
Q.2. a. Menachem Amir. *Patterns in Forcible Rape.*
b. p. 336

Q.3. a. A. T. Carter. *Elite Politics in Rural India: Political Stratification and Political Alliances in Western Maharashtra.*
b. p. 246
Q.4. a. American Medical Association, Council on Drugs
1971 *AMA Drug Evaluations.* 1st ed. Chicago: American Medical Association.
b. vol. 24, p. 520

CHAPTER SEVEN
Q.2. a. 118:B9-11; 26:G4
b. "The Volatile Busing Issue: How It Affects Campaigning"
Q.3. a. Justice Dept files 1st housing-discrimination suit, charging Daniel F Mason of Mobile, Ala, with discriminating against Vietnamese refugee in operation of Mason's Mobile Home Ct in Mobile; suit asks ct to issue injunction forbidding Mason to engage in housing discrimination (S)
b. July 27, p. 11, column 1
Q.4. a. Kanti C. Kotecha and James L. Walker
b. Wright State University

CHAPTER EIGHT
Q.2. a. Karl Schuessler
b. Indiana University
c. Methodology session of the 1972 American Sociological Association meeting in New Orleans
Q.3. a. "Industrial Conflict and Unionization"
b. Blauner, Robert
1964 Alienation and Freedom. Chicago: University of Chicago Press.
Q.4. a. Felix Berardo
b. University of Florida
c. pp. 143-44
Q.5. a. *Abstracts for Social Workers*
b. p. 811

CHAPTER NINE
Q.2. *Social Forces,* 53:143, S '74. W. C. Roof
Q.3. a. Samuel C. Heilman
b. Queens College/CUNY
c. pp. 285-86

CHAPTER TEN
Q.2. a. S241-19
b. p. 659
c. James L. Pate, Asst Sec for Economic Aff, Commerce Dept
Q.3. a. (70) 8284
b. "Administration and Conduct of Antipoverty Programs, Hearings, 91st Congress, 1st Session." 1969. 402 p.

CHAPTER ELEVEN
Q.2. a. 25368-43
b. p. 151
Q.3. a. p. 106
b. 151 p.

MATERIALS & METHODS FOR
SOCIOLOGY RESEARCH

Answers by Book

Book No. __3__

CHAPTER ONE

Q.2. a. *A Glossary of American Technical Linguistic Usage, 1925-1950*
b. p. 286
Q.3. a. *Sociological Abstracts*
b. p. 263

CHAPTER TWO

Q.2. a. vol. 1, p. 488
b. Allen, V. L.
1965 "Conformity and the role of deviant." Journal of Personality 33:584-97.
Q.3. a. 3,487
b. p. 22
Q.4. a. 36.0%
b. 13.9%

CHAPTER THREE

Q.2. a. 2.23 per 1,000 population
b. p. 428
Q.3. a. 14.7 per 1,000 population
b. 48.7 per 1,000 population
c. p. 79
Q.4. a. 99.7
b. 29.7
c. pp. 157-58
Q.5. a. Gary T. Marx and James L. Wood. *Strands of Theory and Research in Collective Behavior.*
b. D. F. Aberle
c. vol. 1, p. 363

CHAPTER FOUR

Q.2. a. *Voting: A Study of Opinion Formation in a Presidential Campaign*
b. vol. 3, p. 522
Q.3. a. Vincent de Gournay
b. p. 20

CHAPTER FIVE

Q.3. a. Fox, G. L.
1975 "Love match and arranged marriage in a modernizing nation: mate selection in Ankara, Turkey." Journal of Marriage and the Family 37:180.
b. p. 529
Q.4. a. "Impact of Urban Migration on Rural Development: Theoretical Considerations and Emperical Evidence from Southern Nigeria"
b. p. 304
Q.5. a. William J. Bowers and Richard G. Salem. "Severity of Formal Sanctions as a Repressive Response to Deviant Behavior"
b. p. 397
Q.6. a. "Forcible Rape: Institutionalized Sexism in the Criminal Justice System"
b. p. 334
Q.7. H. R. Lantz, J. Keyes, and M. Schultz. "American Family in Preindustrial Period—From Base Lines in History to Change"

CHAPTER SIX

Q.2. a. Sharol Rae Cannon. *Social Functioning Patterns in Families of Offspring Receiving Treatment for Drug Abuse.*
b. p. 114
Q.3. a. J. Freeman. "Political Organization in the Feminist Movement"
b. p. 165
Q.4. a. McKnight, Gerald
1973 Computer Crime. London: Joseph.
b. vol. 98, p. 478

CHAPTER SEVEN

Q.2. a. 49:E13-14; 71:E8
b. "Putnam Included in School Bias Plan"
Q.3. a. James Tuite article on ocean cruise ships employing women croupiers; career of croupier Inga Angel noted
b. January 11, p. 46, column 1
Q.4. a. William Alonso
b. University of California, Berkeley

CHAPTER EIGHT

Q.2. a. Wade Clark Roof
b. University of Massachusetts
c. Meeting of the Southern Sociological Society, Atlanta, Georgia, April 1973
Q.3. a. "Household Complexity in Nineteenth Century France"
b. Ackerman, Charles
1963 "Affiliations, structural determinants of differential divorce rates." American Journal of Sociology 69:13-20.
Q.4. a. N. Krishnan Namboodiri
b. University of North Carolina at Chapel Hill
c. pp. 317-18
Q.5. a. *British Humanities Index*
b. p. 812

CHAPTER NINE

Q.2. *American Political Science Review,* 68:1364-5, S'74. S. Chodak.
Q.3. a. Gary Kleck
b. University of Illinois, Urbana
c. pp. 291-93

CHAPTER TEN

Q.2. a. S641-43.4
b. p. 952
c. William Upchurch, project dir, Southwestern Child Dev Commission, Sylva, NC
Q.3. a. (69) 10605
b. "Characteristics of Families and Persons Living in Metropolitan Poverty Areas, 1967." 1969. 16 p.

CHAPTER ELEVEN

Q.2. a. 2546-1.297
b. p. 6
Q.3. a. p. 99
b. 19 p.

MATERIALS & METHODS FOR
SOCIOLOGY RESEARCH

Answers by Book

Book No. 4

CHAPTER ONE

Q.2. a. *A Dictionary of Literary, Dramatic, and Cinematic
Terms*
b. p. 296
Q.3. a. *Abstracts for Social Workers*
b. p. 264

CHAPTER TWO

Q.2. a. vol. 1, p. 568
b. Abegglin, J. C.
1958   The Japanese Factory: Aspects of Its
Social Organization. Glencoe, Ill.: Free
Press.
Q.3. a. 4,360
b. p. 22
Q.4. a. 30.0%
b. 5.0%

CHAPTER THREE

Q.2. a. 2.07 per 1,000 population
b. p. 428
Q.3. a. 14.7 per 1,000 population
b. 49.3 per 1,000 population
c. p. 79
Q.4. a. 213.6
b. 42.4
c. p. 157
Q.5. a. Joan Aldous. *Family Interaction Patterns.*
b. J. Aldous and R. Hill
c. vol. 3, p. 105

CHAPTER FOUR

Q.2. a. *Centuries of Childhood: A Social History of
Family Life*
b. vol. 1, p. 95
Q.3. a. Aristotle
b. p. 26

CHAPTER FIVE

Q.3. a. Jacobs, J. B. and E. H. Steele
1975   "Prisons: instruments of law enforcement
or social welfare?" Crime and Delinquency
21:348-5.
b. p. 688
Q.4. a. *Migration, Income and Employment: Canada,
1965-68. A Special Study of the C. D. Howe
Research Institute (Montreal)*
b. p. 112
Q.5. a. Kurt W. Back and Linda Brookover Bourque.
"Can Feelings be Enumerated?"
b. p. 4
Q.6. a. *Trends in Disorders, Disruptions, and Crimes in
Public Secondary Schools: 1950 to 1975*
b. p. 185
Q.7. P. B. Hoffman and J. L. Back. "Parole Decision-
making—Salient Factor Score"

CHAPTER SIX

Q.2. a. Benjamin J. Sadock (and others), ed.
Sexual Experience.
b. p. 364
Q.3. a. P. A. Back and K. Jennings. "Parents as 'Middle-
Persons' in Political Socialization"
b. p. 247
Q.4. a. Noland, Robert L.
1972   Counseling Parents of the Emotionally
Disturbed Child. Springfield, Ill.: Thomas.
b. vol. 59, p. 405

CHAPTER SEVEN

Q.2. a. 13:G7-8; 2:G2
b. "Governor Confronts Welfare Cut Protest"
Q.3. a. Ed lauds Sargent Shriver for making strengthening
of families a major theme of his Pres candidate
campaign
b. January 17, p. 24, column 2
Q.4. a. David C. Schwartz
b. Livingston College

CHAPTER EIGHT

Q.2. a. Adeline Levine and Janice Crumrine
b. State Univerity of New York at Buffalo
c. American Sociological Association meeting,
New York, August 1973
Q.3. a. "Developmental Change in the Sentiment
Structure of Children's Groups"
b. Atwood, George
1969   "A developmental study of cognitive
balancing in hypothetical three person
system." Child Development 40:73-85.
Q.4. a. Joel Smith
b. Duke University
c. pp. 513-14
Q.5. a. *Social Sciences Citation Index*
b. p. 814

CHAPTER NINE

Q.2. *American Journal of Sociology,* 80:244-7, J1 '74.
A. L. Jacobson.
Q.3. a. Evalyn J. Michaelson
b. California State University, Northridge
c. pp. 151-52

CHAPTER TEN

Q.2. a. H521-34.7
b. p. 341
c. David Carliner, atty, ACLU
Q.3. a. (69) 12402
b. "Business and OEO, Partnership Against Poverty."
1969. 24 p.

CHAPTER ELEVEN

Q.2. a. 6504-1
b. p. 27
Q.3. a. p. 106
b. 62 p.

MATERIALS & METHODS FOR
SOCIOLOGY RESEARCH

Answers by Book

Book No. __5__

CHAPTER ONE

Q.2. a. *The Amateur Astronomer's Glossary*
b. p. 715
Q.3. a. *International Bibliography of Sociology*
b. p. 266

CHAPTER TWO

Q.2. a. vol. 5, p. 602
b. Ackerman, N. W. and Marie Johoda
1950   Anti-Semitism and Emotional Disorder.
New York: Harper.
Q.3. a. 6,761
b. p. 22
Q.4. a. 22.3%
b. 3.5%

CHAPTER THREE

Q.2. a. 0.28 per 1,000 population
b. p. 428
Q.3. a. 14.7 per 1,000 population
b. 42.9 per 1,000 population
c. p. 79
Q.4. a. 61.9
b. 14.8
c. pp. 157-58
Q.5. a. Tom Bottomore. *Competing Paradigms in
Macrosociology.*
b. R. Aron
c. vol. 1, p. 191

CHAPTER FOUR

Q.2. a. *Party and Society: The Anglo-American
Democracies*
b. vol. 1, p. 300
Q.3. a. Jacob L. Moreno
b. p. 205

CHAPTER FIVE

Q.3. a. Felson, M. and M. Solaun
1975   "Fertility—inhibiting effect of crowded
apartment living in a tight housing
market." American Journal of Sociology
80:1410-27.
b. p. 707
Q.4. a. "The Population of the Arab Republic of Egypt.
Part 2. Population Distribution and Internal
Migration and the Labor Force"
b. p. 239
Q.5. a. H. Merrill Jackson. "Social Progress and Mental
Health"
b. p. 273
Q.6. a. "Battered Wives: An Emerging Social Problem"
b. p. 89
Q.7. C. Hendrick, M. Giesen, and R. Borden. "False
Physiological Feedback and Persuasion—Effect of
Fear Arousal vs. Fear Reduction on Attitude-change"

CHAPTER SIX

Q.2. a. Robert Graham Caldwell and James A. Black.
Juvenile Delinquency.
b. p. 218
Q.3. a. J. C. McCann. "Differential Mortality and the
Formation of Political Elites: The Case of the
US House of Representatives"
b. p. 129
Q.4. a. Ackerley, Joe Randolph
1969   My Father and Myself. New York:
Coward-McCann.
b. vol. 42, p. 90

CHAPTER SEVEN

Q.2. a. 37:E14-F2; 8:F4
b. "Credit for Police-community Job Stretches
All the Way to the Bank"
Q.3. a. NYS officials indicate Office of Drug Abuse,
criticized in recent mos for excessive spending,
may be merged with Div of Alcoholism as part
of Gov Hugh Carey's promised overhaul of drug
addiction program; . . .
b. January 4, p. 26, column 1
Q.4. a. J. S. Fuerst
b. Loyola University

CHAPTER EIGHT

Q.2. a. Claude S. Fischer
b. University of California, Berkeley
c. American Sociological Association in New York City
in 1973
Q.3. a. "Heterogamy, Inter-class Mobility and Socio-political
Attitudes in Italy"
b. Arensberg, Conrad M. and S. T. Kimball
1940   Family and Community in Ireland.
Cambridge: Harvard University Press.
Q.4. a. Toyomasa Fusé
b. University of Montreal
c. p. 654-55
Q.5. a. *Public Affairs Information Service*
b. p. 814

CHAPTER NINE

Q.2. *Social Forces*, 53:131, S '74. R. H. Turner
Q.3. a. Janet G. Hunt
b. University of Maryland, College Park
c. pp. 172-73

CHAPTER TEN

Q.2. a. S521-52
b. p. 859
c. James L. Buckley (Sen, C, R-NY)
Q.3. a. (65) 7289
b. "Children and Poverty." 1965. 7 p.

CHAPTER ELEVEN

Q.2. a. 6264-2.1
b. p. 31
Q.3. a. p. 109
b. 38 p.

MATERIALS & METHODS FOR
SOCIOLOGY RESEARCH

Answers by Book

Book No. ___6___

CHAPTER ONE

Q.2. a. *The Condensed Chemical Dictionary*
      b. p. 737
Q.3. a. *Bibliographic Survey: The Negro in Print*
      b. p. 267

CHAPTER TWO

Q.2. a. vol. 2, p. 1
      b. Abelson, R. P. and J. C. Miller
         1967   "Negative persuasion via personal insult."
                Journal of Experimental Social Psychology
                3:321-33.
Q.3. a. 8,627
      b. p. 22
Q.4. a. 46.6%
      b. 13.1%

CHAPTER THREE

Q.2. a. 0.22 per 1,000 population
      b. p. 428
Q.3. a. 14.7 per 1,000 population
      b. 47.8 per 1,000 population
      c. p. 80
Q.4. a. 100.9
      b. 23.9
      c. pp. 157-58
Q.5. a. David Mechanic. *The Comparative Study of Health
         Care Delivery Systems.*
      b. B. Abel-Smith
      c. vol. 1, p. 43

CHAPTER FOUR

Q.2. a. *White and Coloured: The Behavior of British People
         Toward Coloured Immigrants*
      b. vol. 1, p. 443
Q.3. a. Karl Marx/Marxism
      b. p. 31

CHAPTER FIVE

Q.3. a. Sandhu, H. S. and D. E. Allen
         1974   "Family planning in rural India: personal
                and community factors." Journal of
                Marriage and the Family 36:805-13.
      b. p. 65
Q.4. a. "Internal Migration and Economic Development
         in Brazil"
      b. p. 296
Q.5. a. Keith K. Cox. "Social Effects of Integrated
         Advertising"
      b. p. 123
Q.6. a. "The Case Against Capital Punishment"
      b. p. 224
Q.7. J. Freeman. "Political Organization in Feminist
      Movement"

CHAPTER SIX

Q.2. a. Otto Newman. *Gambling: Hazard and Reward.*
      b. p. 182
Q.3. a. J. Armstrong. "Canadians in Crisis: The Nature and
         Source of Support for Leadership in a National
         Emergency"
      b. p. 210
Q.4. a. Gray, Francis Calley
         1973   Prison Discipline in America. Montclair,
                N. J.: Patterson Smith.
      b. vol. 73, p. 70

CHAPTER SEVEN

Q.2. a. 57:G8; 125:D6-7
      b. "Commission Hears Minority Protests Against Police"
Q.3. a. Hundreds line up at special information counters,
         Sydney, Australia, to take advantage of new law
         under which only ground for divorce is irretrievable
         breakdown of a marriage after a 12-mo separation;
         provisions of law cited (S)
      b. January 7, p. 46, column 1
Q.4. a. René Lemarchand
      b. University of Florida

CHAPTER EIGHT

Q.2. a. Ralph H. Turner
      b. University of California, Los Angeles
      c. Meeting of the American Sociological Association
         in Denver, August 1971
Q.3. a. "Cumulative Sociological Knowledge"
      b. Blalock, Hubert M.
         1969   Theory Construction. Englewood Cliffs,
                New Jersey: Prentice-Hall.
Q.4. a. Leonard I. Pearlin
      b. National Institute of Mental Health
      c. pp. 403-04
Q.5. a. *Psychological Abstracts*
      b. p. 816

CHAPTER NINE

Q.2. *Social Forces*, 52:440-1, Mr '74. C. R. Tittle.
Q.3. a. Richard A. Zeller
      b. Bowling Green State University
      c. pp. 183-84

CHAPTER TEN

Q.2. a. H761-4.1
      b. p. 435
      c. Rufus H. Wilson, Chief Benefits Dir, VA
Q.3. a. (66) 17801
      b. "Seminar on Manpower Policy and Program:
         Church and Antipoverty Program." 1966. 21 p.

CHAPTER ELEVEN

Q.2. a. 4278-6
      b. pp. 3-24
Q.3. a. p. 104
      b. 101 p.

MATERIALS & METHODS FOR
SOCIOLOGY RESEARCH

Answers by Book

Book No. ___7___

CHAPTER ONE

Q.2. a. *A Dictionary of Geology*
b. p. 748
Q.3. a. *Sociological Measurement: An Inventory of Scales and Indices*
b. p. 269

CHAPTER TWO

Q.2. a. vol. 2, p. 357
b. Alger, C. F.
1966 "Interaction in a committee of the United Nations General Assembly." Midwest Journal of Political Science 10:411-47.
Q.3. a. 51
b. p. 22
Q.4. a. 31.5%
b. 6.6%

CHAPTER THREE

Q.2. a. 1.37 per 1,000 population
b. p. 429
Q.3. a. 14.7 per 1,000 population
b. 18.1 per 1,000 population
c. p. 80
Q.4. a. 108.3
b. 38.9
c. p. 157
Q.5. a. W. Richard Scott. *Organizational Structure.*
b. G. T. Allison
c. vol. 1, p. 1

CHAPTER FOUR

Q.2. a. *My Mother Who Fathered Me: A Study of the Family in Three Selected Communities in Jamaica*
b. vol. 2, p. 318
Q.3. a. Emile Durkheim
b. p. 32

CHAPTER FIVE

Q.3. a. Brieland, D.
1974 "Children and families: a forecast." Social Work 19:568-79.
b. p. 100
Q.4. a. "Census Data on Internal Migration in Southeast Asia and Australia: Limitation and Opportunities"
b. p. 525
Q.5. a. Timothy R. L. Black. "A Survey of Contraceptive Markets in Four African Countries"
b. p. 367
Q.6. a. "Changing Alienations as Consequences of Imprisonment"
b. p. 59
Q.7. J. Kellerha. "Family Dimensions of Stratification"

CHAPTER SIX

Q.2. a. Richard H. Blum and others. *Horatio Alger's Children (The Role of the Family in the Origin and Prevention of Drug Risk).*
b. p. 129

Q.3. a. L. N. Stern, L. D. Dobson and F. P. Scioli. "On the Dimensions of Political Culture: A New Perspective"
b. p. 213
Q.4. a. Keller, Oliver J. and Benedict S. Alper
1970 Halfway Houses: Community-centered Correction and Treatment. Lexington, Mass.: Heath Lexington Books.
b. vol. 50, p. 284

CHAPTER SEVEN

Q.2. a. 93:G2-3; 8:F4
b. "D.C. Police Gain in Esteem; Some Area Forces Decline"
Q.3. a. Jury hears tape recordings of alleged conversations between L F Taylor and Sen-elect Rodriguez, NYC; . . .
b. January 4, p. 28, column 3
Q.4. a. Harry Howe Ransom
b. Vanderbilt University

CHAPTER EIGHT

Q.2. a. Mark Granovetter
b. Harvard University
c. Mont Chateau conference on the anthropological study of social networks
Q.3. a. "Role-taking and Power in Social Psychology"
b. Blood, R. O. and D. M. Wolfe
1960 Husbands and Wives: The Dynamics of Married Living. Glenco, Illinois: The Free Press.
Q.4. a. Robert O. Blood, Jr.
b. Pendle Hill
c. pp. 404-05
Q.5. a. *Biological Abstracts*
b. p. 816

CHAPTER NINE

Q.2. *American Journal of Sociology,* 80:271-3, J1 '74. V. Gecas.
Q.3. a. Yolanda T. Wesely
b. Office of Social Research Equitable Life Assurance Society, New York City
c. pp. 66-67

CHAPTER TEN

Q.2. a. H341-43.3
b. p. 190
c. Joseph F. Bass, Jr., pres, ACTION Employees' Union, Local 2027, Amer Fedn of State, Cty and Municipal Employees
Q.3. a. (66) 4299
b. "Education, Answer to Poverty, School Programs Which May Be Eligible for Federal Aid." 1965. 76 p.

CHAPTER ELEVEN

Q.2. a. 2308-36
b. pp. 156-67
Q.3. a. p. 109
b. 38 p.

MATERIALS & METHODS FOR
SOCIOLOGY RESEARCH

Answers by Book

Book No. _8_

CHAPTER ONE

Q.2. a. *An Etymological Dictionary of Chemistry and Mineralogy*
b. p. 753

Q.3. a. *Directory: State and Federal Correctional Institutions of the United States of America, Canada, England and Scotland*
b. p. 289

CHAPTER TWO

Q.2. a. vol. 2, p. 526
b. American Psychological Association
1954   Ethical Standards for Psychologists. Washington, D. C.: American Psychological Association.

Q.3. a. 292
b. p. 22

Q.4. a. 16.7%
b. 5.5%

CHAPTER THREE

Q.2. a. 0.22 per 1,000 population
b. p. 429

Q.3. a. 14.7 per 1,000 population
b. 25.4 per 1,000 population
c. p. 80

Q.4. a. 51.3
b. 25.7
c. pp. 157-58

Q.5. a. Jack P. Gibbs and Maynard L. Erickson. *Major Developments in the Sociological Study of Deviance.*
b. H. S. Becker
c. vol. 1, p. 21

CHAPTER FOUR

Q.2. a. *A Fragment on Government*
b. vol. 2, p. 486

Q.3. a. Patrick Geddes
b. p. 43

CHAPTER FIVE

Q.3. a. Ramsy, N. R.
1974   "Assortative mating and the structure of cities." American Sociological Review 31:773-86.
b. p. 108

Q.4. a. "Rural-Urban Migration, Urban Underemployment and Earnings Differentials in Pakistan"
b. p. 114

Q.5. a. T. G. McGee. "Peasants in the Cities: A Paradox, A Paradox, A Most Ingenious Paradox"
b. p. 951

Q.6. a. "Vandalism"
b. p. 66

Q.7. Z. F. Gamson. "Group-process and Organizational Environment—Student Organization in University"

CHAPTER SIX

Q.2. a. David Lester. *Unusual Sexual Behavior: The Standard Deviations.*
b. p. 434

Q.3. a. D. R. Segal and D. Knoke. "The Impact of Social Stratification, Social Mobility, and Status Inconsistency on the German Political Party Infrastructure"
b. p. 106

Q.4. a. Becker, Russell J.
1971   When Marriage Ends. Philadelphia: Fortress Press.
b. vol. 24, p. 174

CHAPTER SEVEN

Q.2. a. 10:B12; 47:B7-9
b. "27 Women Graduate in 1st CHP Coed Class"

Q.3. a. NYS Bar Assn plans study to find 'more sensible' ways of dealing with alcoholics; assn pres Tondel says alcoholism is soc offense that could be removed from ct system to be handled in other ways
b. February 1, p. 60, column 1

Q.4. a. Richard C. U'Ren
b. University of Oregon Health Sciences Center

CHAPTER EIGHT

Q.2. a. Alejandro Portes
b. Duke University
c. Comparative Urbanization Seminar, Northwestern University, January 1975

Q.3. a. "A Theory of Ethnic Antagonism: The Split Labor Market"
b. Bailey, Thomas A.
1934   Theodore Roosevelt and the Japanese-American Crises. Stanford: Stanford University Press.

Q.4. a. Joe R. Feagin
b. University of Texas at Austin
c. p. 536-37

Q.5. a. *Social Sciences Citation Index*
b. p. 817

CHAPTER NINE

Q.2. *International Journal of Comparative Sociology*, 15:225-6, S/N '74. J. A. Nagata.

Q.3. a. Hanan C. Selvin
b. SUNY/Stony Brook
c. pp. 62-64

CHAPTER TEN

Q.2. a. H521-10.7
b. p. 334
c. Aryeh Neier, exec dir, ACLU

Q.3. a. (66) 10877
b. "Employed Poor, Their Characteristics and Occupations." 1966. pp. 828-41.

CHAPTER ELEVEN

Q.2. a. 4824-15
b. p. 4

Q.3. a. p. 110
b. 73 p.

MATERIALS & METHODS FOR
SOCIOLOGY RESEARCH

Answers by Book

Book No. __9__

CHAPTER ONE

Q.2. a. *Harvard Dictionary of Music*
b. p. 420
Q.3. a. *Elsevier's Dictionary of Criminal Science in Eight
Languages*
b. p. 292

CHAPTER TWO

Q.2. a. vol. 2, p. 596
b. Abcarian, G. and S. M. Stange
1965 "Alienation and the radical right." Journal
of Politics 27:776-96.
Q.3. a. 859
b. p. 22
Q.4. a. 20.3%
b. 4.8%

CHAPTER THREE

Q.2. a. 0.87 per 1,000 population
b. p. 429
Q.3. a. 14.7 per 1,000 population
b. 19.2 per 1,000 population
c. p. 80
Q.4. a. 79.7
b. 31.0
c. pp. 157-58
Q.5. a. Jeylan T. Mortimer and Roberta G. Simmons.
Adult Socialization.
b. R. C. Atchley
c. vol. 4, p. 421

CHAPTER FOUR

Q.2. a. *Modern Theories of Criminality*
b. vol. 3, p. 509
Q.3. a. P. Topinard
b. p. 45

CHAPTER FIVE

Q.3. a. Tittle, C. R. and A. R. Rowe
1974 "Certainty of arrest and crime rates:
a further test of the deterrence
hypothesis." Social Forces 52:455-62.
b. p. 150
Q.4. a. "Internal Migration and Structural Changes in
Egypt"
b. p. 92
Q.5. a. John B. McConahay and Joseph C. Hough, Jr.
"Love and Guilt-oriented Dimension of Christian
Belief"
b. p. 1148
Q.6. a. *Developing Citizen Action for Marijuana Law Reform*
b. p. 12
Q.7. R. P. Allen, R. Heaton, and M. Barrell. "Behavior-
therapy for Socially Ineffective Children"

CHAPTER SIX

Q.2. a. Nancy Gager and Cathleen Schurr. *Sexual Assault:
Confronting Rape in America.*
b. p. 399
Q.3. a. L. A. Stone and G. J. Coles. "Multidimensional
Judgment Scaling of Well-known Political Figures"
b. p. 28
Q.4. a. Stuart, Irving R.
1972 Children of Separation and Divorce.
New York: Grossman.
b. vol. 14, p. 545

CHAPTER SEVEN

Q.2. a. 72:C10-11; 38:E14
b. "SP Sex Discrimination Issue Not Settled"
Q.3. a. Violence and crime become dominant factors in
Haight-Ashbury sec of San Francisco, change
character of neighborhood
b. January 5, p. 46, column 3
Q.4. a. Cathy S. Greenblat
b. Douglass College, Rutgers University

CHAPTER EIGHT

Q.2. a. Gudmund Hernes
b. University of Bergen
c. Meeting of the International Sociological Association
in Toronto, 1974, and at the Mathematical Social
Science Board conference in St. Louis, 1975
Q.3. a. "Race, Class, and Consciousness"
b. Allen, Irving L. and J. David Colfax
1968 Urban Problems and Public Opinion in
Four Connecticut Cities. Storrs: Institute
of Urban Research.
Q.4. a. Walter A. Sedelow, Jr.
b. University of Kansas
c. p. 277
Q.5. a. *Abstracts for Social Workers*
b. p. 818

CHAPTER NINE

Q.2. *American Anthropologist,* 76:881-2, D'74.
L. D. Borman.
Q.3. a. Conrad C. Vogler
b. SUNY/Buffalo
c. p. 48

CHAPTER TEN

Q.2. a. S181-73.13
b. p. 738
c. Morris Thompson, Commr of Indian Aff, BIA
Q.3. a. (68) 10026
b. "Extent of Poverty in the United States 1959-66."
1968. 32 p.

CHAPTER ELEVEN

Q.2. a. 6504-1
b. p. 29
Q.3. a. p. 98
b. 6 p.

MATERIALS & METHODS FOR
SOCIOLOGY RESEARCH

Answers by Book

Book No. __10__

CHAPTER ONE

Q.2.　a. *Dictionary of French Literature*
　　　b. p. 351
Q.3.　a. *Encyclopedia of Social Work: Successor to the Social Work Yearbook*
　　　b. p. 294

CHAPTER TWO

Q.2.　a. vol. 2, p. 693
　　　b. Acherman, C.
　　　　　1963　"Affiliations: structural determinants of differential divorce rates." American Journal of Sociology 69:13-20.
Q.3.　a. 1,610
　　　b. p. 22
Q.4.　a. 21.8%
　　　b. 4.5%

CHAPTER THREE

Q.2.　a. 1.04 per 1,000 population
　　　b. p. 429
Q.3.　a. 14.7 per 1,000 population
　　　b. 49.3 per 1,000 population
　　　c. p. 80
Q.4.　a. 52.5
　　　b. 77.8
　　　c. p. 157
Q.5.　a. Robin M. Williams, Jr. *Race and Ethnic Relations.*
　　　b. H. Adam
　　　c. vol. 1, p. 125

CHAPTER FOUR

Q.2.　a. *Man and Society in Disaster*
　　　b. vol. 4, p. 155
Q.3.　a. E. B. Tylor
　　　b. p. 46

CHAPTER FIVE

Q.3.　a. Weed, J. A.
　　　　　1974　"Age at marriage as a factor in state divorce rate differentials." Demography 11:361-75.
　　　b. p. 172
Q.4.　a. *Black Internal Migration, U. S. and Ghana: A Comparative Study*
　　　b. p. 270
Q.5.　a. Michio Kitahara. "A Function of Marriage Ceremony"
　　　b. p. 1270
Q.6.　a. *Caged: Eight Prisoners and Their Keepers*
　　　b. p. 48
Q.7.　T. J. Labelle and R. E. Verhine. "Nonformal Education and Occupational Stratification—Implications for Latin-America"

CHAPTER SIX

Q.2.　a. Richard J. Gelles. *Violent Home: A Study of Physical Aggression Between Husbands and Wives.*
　　　b. p. 103
Q.3.　a. W. A. Welsh. "Methodological Problems in the Study of Political Leadership in Latin America"
　　　b. p. 197
Q.4.　a. Denney, Anthony Howe
　　　　　1973　When Father is Away. London: Priory Press.
　　　b. vol. 31, p. 295

CHAPTER SEVEN

Q.2.　a. 29:C6; 38:F4
　　　b. "2 Women Among 22 New Black Troopers"
Q.3.　a. Cairo police begin crackdown on pickpockets
　　　b. April 9, p. 8, column 5
Q.4.　a. Emile G. McAnany
　　　b. Stanford University

CHAPTER EIGHT

Q.2.　a. Leonard Broom and F. Lancaster Jones
　　　b. Australian National University
　　　c. Eighth World Congress of Sociology, Toronto, 1974
Q.3.　a. "Differentials in Marital Instability: 1970"
　　　b. Blood, Robert O., Jr. and Donald M. Wolfe
　　　　　1960　Husbands and Wives: The Dynamics of Married Living. New York: The Free Press.
Q.4.　a. Howard W. Polsky
　　　b. Columbia University
　　　c. pp. 285-86
Q.5.　a. *Abstracts for Social Workers*
　　　b. p. 818

CHAPTER NINE

Q.2.　*Social Forces,* 53:660-1, Je '75. C. R. Hofstetter.
Q.3.　a. Gary G. Hamilton
　　　b. University of California, Davis
　　　c. pp. 53-54

CHAPTER TEN

Q.2.　a. S181-34.6
　　　b. p. 699
　　　c. William D. Gilbert, Dep Dir of Engineering and Services, USAF
Q.3.　a. (69) 15477
　　　b. "Food Gap, Poverty and Malnutrition in United States Interim Report Together With Supplemental, Additional, and Individual Views." 1969. 48 p.

CHAPTER ELEVEN

Q.2.　a. 6404-2.2
　　　b. p. 262
Q.3.　a. p. 95
　　　b. 96 p.

MATERIALS & METHODS FOR
SOCIOLOGY RESEARCH

Answers by Book

Book No. 11

CHAPTER ONE

Q.2. a. *A Dictionary of Biology*
b. p. 719
Q.3. a. *Handbook of Small Group Research*
b. p. 295

CHAPTER TWO

Q.2. a. vol. 3, p. 50
b. Adams, J. S.
1961 "Reduction of cognitive dissonance by
seeking consonant information." Journal
of Abnormal Social Psychology 62:74-78.
Q.3. a. 3,352
b. p. 22
Q.4. a. 24.8%
b. 8.2%

CHAPTER THREE

Q.2. a. 1.11 per 1,000 population
b. p. 429
Q.3. a. 14.7 per 1,000 population
b. 29.8 per 1,000 population
c. p. 80
Q.4. a. 74.7
b. 89.9
c. pp. 157-58
Q.5. a. William Peterson. *International Migration.*
b. B. E. Aguivre
c. vol. 4, p. 533

CHAPTER FOUR

Q.2. a. *Family and Community in Ireland*
b. vol. 4, p. 505
Q.3. a. A. Guillard
b. p. 52

CHAPTER FIVE

Q.3. a. Taylor, B. K.
1975 "Absence of sociological and structural
problem focus in community studies."
European Journal of Sociology 16:296-309.
b. p. 868
Q.4. a. *Some Aspects of Migration Among Women in Lagos*
b. p. 229
Q.5. a. E. D. Wittkower and Guy Dubreuil. "Psychocultural
Stress in Relation to Mental Illness"
b. p. 501
Q.6. a. *Human Factors and Employee Attitudes*
b. p. 358
Q.7. R. G. Iacovett. "Adolescent-Adult Interaction and
Peer-group Involvement"

CHAPTER SIX

Q.2. a. Don Cahalan and Robin Room. *Problem Drinking
Among American Men.*
b. p. 14

Q.3. a. M. Seeman. "The Signals of 68: Alienation in
Pre-crisis France"
b. p. 62
Q.4. a. Coffey, Alan
1974 Juvenile Justice as a System: Law
Enforcement to Rehabilitation. Englewood
Cliffs, N. J.: Prentice-Hall.
b. vol. 76, p. 268

CHAPTER SEVEN

Q.2. a. 10:C7; 113:D1
b. "First Woman Trooper Ready to Start Work"
Q.3. a. 3 Kennebec County Jail inmates go on rampage;
talked into submission by police
b. December 26, p. 41, column 7
Q.4. a. Barbara Carter
b. Federal City College, Washington, D. C.

CHAPTER EIGHT

Q.2. a. Paul Burstein and William Freudenburg
b. Yale University
c. Annual meeting of the American Sociological
Association, New York, August 1976
Q.3. a. "Loss of Power"
b. Arendt, Hannah
1951 The Origins of Totalitarianism.
New York: Harcourt Brace.
Q.4. a. Stephen Cole
b. State University of New York at Stony Brook
c. pp. 548-49
Q.5. a. *Public Affairs Information Service*
b. p. 818

CHAPTER NINE

Q.2. *American Journal of Sociology,* 80:1475-7, My '75.
T. Koenig.
Q.3. a. Mark Tannenbaum
b. Harvard Law School and University of Michigan,
Ann Arbor
c. pp. 67-68

CHAPTER TEN

Q.2. a. H521-28.4
b. p. 381
c. Ronna I. Wineburg, atty, Colo Rural Legal Services
Q.3. a. (66) 11319
b. "Growing Up Poor, Over-view and Analysis of
Child-rearing and Family Life Pattern Associated
with Poverty." 1966. 117 p.

CHAPTER ELEVEN

Q.2. a. 1804-8
b. p. 3
Q.3. a. p. 95
b. 59 p.

MATERIALS & METHODS FOR
SOCIOLOGY RESEARCH

Answers by Book

Book No. _12_

CHAPTER ONE

Q.2. a. *Dictionary of Spanish Literature*
b. p. 359
Q.3. a. *American Jewish Yearbook*
b. p. 298

CHAPTER TWO

Q.2. a. vol. 3, p. 136
b. Abelson, R. P., E. Aronson, W. J. McGuire, T. N.
Newcomb, M. J. Rosenberg, and P. Tannenbaum, eds.
Theories of Cognitive Consistency:
A Sourcebook. Chicago: Rand McNally.
Q.3. a. 5,404
b. p. 22
Q.4. a. 35.5%
b. 5.9%

CHAPTER THREE

Q.2. a. 1.06 per 1,000 population
b. p. 429
Q.3. a. 14.7 per 1,000 population
b. 42.4 per 1,000 population
c. p. 80
Q.4. a. 50.9
b. 77.6
c. pp. 157-58
Q.5. a. Seymour Sudman. *Sample Surveys.*
b. G. A. Almond and S. Verba
c. vol. 2, p. 107

CHAPTER FOUR

Q.2. a. *Elites and Society*
b. vol. 5, p. 29
Q.3. a. Gregory Bateson
b. p. 63

CHAPTER FIVE

Q.3. a. Guzzetta, R. A.
1976   "Acquisition and transfer of empathy
by the parents of early adolescents through
structured learning training." Journal of
Counseling Psychology 23:449-53.
b. p. 281
Q.4. a. "Ethnic Variables in East African Urban Migration"
b. p. 94
Q.5. a. Claudeen Cline Naffziger and Ken Naffziger.
"Development of Sex Role Stereotypes"
b. p. 644
Q.6. a. *An Ecological Analysis of Crime in Rural Ohio*
b. p. 341
Q.7. K. Tominaga and Y. Takada. "Unknown Giant of
Sociology"

CHAPTER SIX

Q.2. a. Lester Grinspoon and Peter Hedblom. *Speed
Culture: Amphetamine Use and Abuse in America.*
b. p. 123

Q.3. a. K. Klare. "The Critique of Everyday Life. Marxism
and the New Left"
b. p. 188
Q.4. a. Cincinnati, University
1968?   The Cincinnati Police-Juvenile Attitude
Project: A Demonstration Project in
Police-Teacher Curriculum Development
to Improve Police-Juvenile Relations.
Washington: Office of Law Enforcement
Assistance, U.S. Dept. of Justice.
b. vol. 71, p. 274

CHAPTER SEVEN

Q.2. a. 48:A14; 138:G14
b. "Massage Parlor Bill Introduced in Legislature"
Q.3. a. 300 prison parolees will be helped to get civilian
jobs under $169,038 on-the-job Fed training program
b. April 7, p. 9, column 1
Q.4. a. A. Dale Tussing
b. Syracuse University

CHAPTER EIGHT

Q.2. a. Andrew J. Weigert and Ross Hastings
b. University of Notre Dame; University of Ottawa
c. Theory Workshop of the National Council of Family
Relations annual meeting, 1973
Q.3. a. "Political Overconformity by Upwardly Mobile
American Men"
b. Butler, D. and D. Stokes
1969   Political Change in Britain.
London: Macmillan.
Q.4. a. Alex Simirenko
b. Pennsylvania State University
c. pp. 140-41
Q.5. a. *Public Affairs Information Service*
b. p. 819

CHAPTER NINE

Q.2. *Social Forces*, 53:658, Je '75. J. Seidler.
Q.3. a. Paul D. Starr
b. Auburn University
c. p. 77

CHAPTER TEN

Q.2. a. S181-52.8
b. p. 717
c. Walter E. Brown, pres, Natl Assn of Neighborhood
Health Centers (NANH); dir NANH center, NYC
Q.3. a. (69) 1315
b. "Housing Conditions in Urban Poverty Areas."
1968. 21 p.

CHAPTER ELEVEN

Q.2. a. 4644-1
b. p. 10
Q.3. a. p. 97
b. 5 p.

MATERIALS & METHODS FOR
SOCIOLOGY RESEARCH

Answers by Book

Book No. __13__

CHAPTER ONE

Q.2. a. *Encyclopaedic Dictionary of Physics: General,
Nuclear, Solid State, Molecular, Chemical, Metal
and Vacuum Physics, Astronomy, Geophysics,
Biophysics, and Related Subjects*
b. p. 765
Q.3. a. *Social Indicators*
b. p. 298

CHAPTER TWO

Q.2. a. vol. 3, p. 450
b. Aberle, D. F.
1961 "Culture and socialization." Pp. 381-99
in F. L. K. Hsu (ed.), Psychological
Anthropology: Approaches to Culture and
Personality. Homewood, Ill.: Dorsey.
Q.3. a. 2,622
b. p. 22
Q.4. a. 29.8%
b. 7.0%

CHAPTER THREE

Q.2. a. 1.41 per 1,000 population
b. p. 429
Q.3. a. 14.7 per 1,000 population
b. 42.0 per 1,000 population
c. p. 80
Q.4. a. 1,623.7
b. 927.4
c. p. 157
Q.5. a. K. P. Moseley. *Precapitalist Social Structures.*
b. R. M. Adams
c. vol. 4, p. 259

CHAPTER FOUR

Q.2. a. *On Human Finery*
b. vol. 5, p. 345
Q.3. a. Sir K. R. Popper
b. p. 70

CHAPTER FIVE

Q.3. a. Cialdini, R. B. and others
1976 "Basking in reflected glory: three (football)
field studies." Journal of Personality and
Social Psychology 34:366-75.
b. p. 379
Q.4. a. "Dynamic Measure of Redistribution of Human
Resources, a Case Study of Indian Census Data
During 1961-1971"
b. p. 53
Q.5. a. David E. Payne. "Alienation: An Organizational-
Societal Comparison"
b. p. 371
Q.6. a. "Mafia: The Prototypical Alien Conspiracy"
b. p. 354
Q.7. M. J. Greenwood. "Research on Internal Migration
in United States—Survey"

CHAPTER SIX

Q.2. a. James Haskins. *Street Gangs: Yesterday and Today.*
b. p. 177
Q.3. a. R. E. Blackwell and W. E. Hulbary. "Political Mobility
Among Soviet Obkom Elites: The Effects of Regime,
Social Backgrounds and Career Development"
b. p. 224
Q.4. a. Brennan, James Joseph and Donald W. Olmsted
1965 Police Work with Delinquents: Analysis
of a Training Program. East Lansing: Social
Science Research Bureau, Michigan State
University.
b. vol. 31, p. 341

CHAPTER SEVEN

Q.2. a. 72:G3-4; 73:A7
b. "Law Against Prostitution is Proposed"
Q.3. a. Franc devaluation brings boom to French casinos
b. January 2, p. 1, column 1
Q.4. a. Fred Barbaro
b. Columbia University

CHAPTER EIGHT

Q.2. a. Jack Goody
b. St. John's College, Cambridge
c. Department of Sociology, University of Chicago, in
May 1969
Q.3. a. "New Directions in the Study of Community Elites"
b. Aiken, Michael and Paul Mott (eds.)
1970 The Structure of Community Power.
New York: Random House.
Q.4. a. Helen M. Lewis
b. Clinch Valley College of the University of Virginia
at Wise
c. pp. 138-40
Q.5. a. *Public Affairs Information Service*
b. p. 819

CHAPTER NINE

Q.2. *Sociology and Social Research,* 59:414-15, J1 '75.
N. Alexander.
Q.3. a. William H. Friedland
b. University of California, Santa Cruz
c. pp. 159-60

CHAPTER TEN

Q.2. a. H181-19.13
b. p. 57
c. Bert A. Gallegos, Dir, Community Service
Admin (CSA)
Q.3. a. (66) 8822 or (65) 16076
b. "Conference Proceedings, National Conference on
Law and Poverty." 1966. 200 p.

CHAPTER ELEVEN

Q.2. a. 4202-4
b. pp. 2-3
Q.3. a. p. 97
b. 5 p.

MATERIALS & METHODS FOR
SOCIOLOGY RESEARCH

Answers by Book

Book No.   14

CHAPTER ONE

Q.2.   a. *Aviation and Space Dictionary*
       b. p. 778
Q.3.   a. *Population of the United States*
       b. p. 299

CHAPTER TWO

Q.2.   a. vol. 3, p. 666
       b. Allport, F. H.
          1924   Social Psychology. Boston: Houghton
                 Mifflin.
Q.3.   a. 3,461
       b. p. 22
Q.4.   a. 28.8%
       b. 4.7%

CHAPTER THREE

Q.2.   a. 1.33 per 1,000 population
       b. p. 429
Q.3.   a. 14.7 per 1,000 population
       b. 42.9 per 1,000 population
       c. p. 82
Q.4.   a. 1,131.7
       b. 642.8
       c. pp. 157-58
Q.5.   a. Aage B. Sorensen. *Mathematical Models in Sociology.*
       b. P. Abell
       c. vol. 4, p. 345

CHAPTER FOUR

Q.2.   a. *Voting: A Study of Opinion Formation in a
          Presidential Campaign*
       b. vol. 6, p. 17
Q.3.   a. W. G. Sumner
       b. p. 71

CHAPTER FIVE

Q.3.   a. Wolff, J.
          1975   "Hermeneutics and the critique of ideology
                 (Frankfort school)." Sociological Review
                 new series 23:811-28.
       b. p. 421
Q.4.   a. *Selective Migration and Population Redistribution:
          A Study of a New Town in Israel*
       b. p. 640
Q.5.   Joe R. Feagin. "Civil Rights Voting by Southern
       Congressmen"
       b. p. 95
Q.6.   a. *The House Prostitute: A Case Study*
       b. p. 364
Q.7.   R. F. Harney. "Padrone and Immigrant"

CHAPTER SIX

Q.2.   a. Frederic Storaska. *How to Say No to a Rapist and
          Survive.*
       b. p. 380

Q.3.   a. T. R. Gurr and R. Duvall. "Civil Conflict in the
          1960s: A Reciprocal Theoretical System"
       b. p. 228
Q.4.   a. Council of Europe, European Committee on Crime
          Problems
             1967   Short-term Methods of Treatment for
                    Young Offenders. Report on Short-term
                    Methods of Treatment for Young
                    Offenders. Strasbourg: Council of Europe.
       b. vol. 33, p. 364

CHAPTER SEVEN

Q.2.   a. 18:F4-5; 18:F6
       b. "Study Asks End of Criminal Sanctions Against
          Prostitution, Drug Addiction"
Q.3.   a. Alaska Gov Jay S Hammond repts plea bargaining
          in criminal cases will end Aug 15 in effort to bolster
          pub confidence in adm of criminal justice; . . .
       b. July 12, p. 8, column 6
Q.4.   a. Dorothy Nelkin
       b. Cornell University

CHAPTER EIGHT

Q.2.   a. Glenn A. Goodwin
       b. Pitzer College
       c. Annual Meetings of the American Sociological
          Association, September 1969, San Francisco,
          California
Q.3.   a. "On Urban Alienations and Anomie: Powerlessness
          and Social Isolation"
       b. Almond, G. and S. Verba
          1963   The Civic Culture. Princeton: Princeton
                 University Press.
Q.4.   a. Irvin Kenneth Zola
       b. Brandeis University
       c. p. 361
Q.5.   a. *ABC Political Science*
       b. p. 819

CHAPTER NINE

Q.2.   *Social Forces*, 54:500, D '75. J. B. Williamson.
Q.3.   a. David Glanz
       b. Columbia University
       c. pp. 165-67

CHAPTER TEN

Q.2.   a. S521-35.4
       b. p. 975
       c. Jane F. Cahill (Dr.), natl dir, Catholics for a
          Free Choice, Ga.
Q.3.   a. (66) 14078
       b. "Low-income Life Styles." 1966. 86 p.

CHAPTER ELEVEN

Q.2.   a. 6504-1
       b. p. 29
Q.3.   a. p. 97
       b. 14 p.

MATERIALS & METHODS FOR
SOCIOLOGY RESEARCH

Answers by Book

Book No. 15

CHAPTER ONE

Q.2. a. *Dictionary of Architecture*
 b. p. 387
Q.3. a. *The Student Sociologist's Handbook*
 b. p. 260

CHAPTER TWO

Q.2. a. vol. 3, p. 853
 b. Alexander, C.
  1960 "A result of visual aesthetics." British
   Journal of Psychology 51:357-71.
Q.3. a. 4,419
 b. p. 22
Q.4. a. 22.6%
 b. 3.5%

CHAPTER THREE

Q.2. a. 2.07 per 1,000 population
 b. p. 429
Q.3. a. 14.7 per 1,000 population
 b. 37.1 per 1,000 population
 c. p. 81
Q.4. a. 1,520.0
 b. 757.4
 c. pp. 157-58
Q.5. a. Howard Schuman and Michael P. Johnson.
  Attitudes and Behavior.
 b. R. P. Abelson
 c. vol. 2, p. 161

CHAPTER FOUR

Q.2. a. *Illiteracy in the Several Countries of the World*
 b. vol. 9, p. 417
Q.3. a. J. S. Mill
 b. p. 72

CHAPTER FIVE

Q.3. a. Taylor, D. G.
  1976 "Accuracy of respondent-coded
   occupation." Public Opinion Quarterly
   40:245-55.
 b. p. 869
Q.4. a. *New Town: A Case Study of Migration to a Growth
  Point in Mid-Wales: Report on 1973 Survey*
 b. p. 474
Q.5. a. Melvin B. Mogulof. "The Character of Advocacy
  in Land Use Control: The Case of California's Coastal
  Zone Commissions"
 b. p. 1017
Q.6. a. "Using Student Volunteers in Anti-rape Programs"
 b. p. 366
Q.7. A. B. Dotson. "Social Planning and Urban Violence—
 Extension of McElroy and Singell"

CHAPTER SIX

Q.2. a. Richard E. Hardy and John G. Cull. *Problems of
  Adolescents: Social and Psychological Approaches.*
 b. p. 246

Q.3. a. S. Gillett. "The Survival of Chieftaincy in Botswana"
 b. p. 224
Q.4. a. Wynn, Margaret
  1964 Fatherless Families: A Study of Families
   Deprived of a Father by Death, Divorce,
   Separation or Desertion Before or After
   Marriage. New York: London House &
   Maxwell.
 b. vol. 14, p. 413

CHAPTER SEVEN

Q.2. a. 10:F3; 10:F10
 b. "Legislator Aims Legal Chop at 'Massage' Parlors"
Q.3. a. 3 Amers, jailed in Cuba for smuggling ton of
  marijuana, return to US; . . .
 b. February 13, p. 14, column 2
Q.4. a. Kurt Weis and Michael E. Milakovich
 b. Universitat des Saarlandes, Saarbruechen, West
  Germany; University of North Carolina

CHAPTER EIGHT

Q.2. a. Denise B. Kandel
 b. Columbia University and New York State
  Department of Mental Hygiene
 c. 64th Annual Meeting of the American Sociological
  Association, San Francisco, September 1969
Q.3. a. "Trends in the Occupational Mobility of U. S. Men,
  1962-1970"
 b. Blau, Peter M. and Otis Dudley Duncan
  1967 The American Occupational Structure.
   New York: John Wiley and Sons, Inc.
Q.4. a. Marion G. Vanfossen
 b. College of William and Mary
 c. pp. 512-13
Q.5. a. *Abstracts for Social Workers*
 b. p. 820

CHAPTER NINE

Q.2. *American Journal of Sociology,* 81:966-8, Ja '76.
  A. T. Scull.
Q.3. a. Robert Sommer
 b. University of California, Davis
 c. pp. 177-78

CHAPTER TEN

Q.2. a. S361-28.14
 b. p. 849
 c. Doris Royal, family farmer, Springfield, Nebr.
Q.3. a. (65) 468
 b. "Poverty in Rural Areas of United States." 1964.
  46 p.

CHAPTER ELEVEN

Q.2. a. 6504-1
 b. p. 39
Q.3. a. p. 97-98
 b. 78 p.

MATERIALS & METHODS FOR
SOCIOLOGY RESEARCH

Answers by Book

Book No. __16__

CHAPTER ONE

Q.2. a. *Elsevier's Dictionary of Chemical Engineering*
     b. p. 781
Q.3. a. *American Journal of Sociology*
     b. p. 261

CHAPTER TWO

Q.2. a. vol. 4, p. 205
     b. Ackerson, L.
       1942   Children's Behavior Problems. Chicago: University of Chicago Press.
Q.3. a. 5,708
     b. p. 22
Q.4. a. 19.9%
     b. 11.1%

CHAPTER THREE

Q.2. a. 2.60 per 1,000 population
     b. p. 429
Q.3. a. 14.7 per 1,000 population
     b. 20.9 per 1,000 population
     c. p. 81
Q.4. a. 382.7
     b. 270.1
     c. p. 157
Q.5. a. Richard D. Schwartz. *Moral Order and Sociology of Law: Trends, Problems, and Prospects.*
     b. T. Arnold
     c. vol. 4, p. 577

CHAPTER FOUR

Q.2. a. *Some Theoretical Aspects of Multiple Decrement Tables*
     b. vol. 9, p. 298
Q.3. a. A. R. Radcliffe-Brown
     b. p. 72

CHAPTER FIVE

Q.3. a. Tracey, D. A. and P. E. Natham
       1976   "Behavioral analysis of chronic alcoholism in four women." Journal of Consulting Clinical Psychology 44:832-42.
     b. p. 25
Q.4. a. *Internal Migration, 1971-1972 (Preliminary Statement)*
     b. p. 91
Q.5. a. Vivian W. Henderson. "Blacks and Change in Higher Education"
     b. p. 402
Q.6. a. *Citizen Patrol Projects: National Evaluation Program Phase I Summary Report*
     b. p. 150
Q.7. L. Driedger. "Doctoral Belief—Major Factor in Differential Perception of Social Issues"

CHAPTER SIX

Q.2. a. Roger F. Aubrey. *Counselor and Drug Abuse Programs.*
     b. p. 114
Q.3. a. A. R. Wilcox (ed.). *Public Opinion and Political Attitudes.*
     b. p. 57
Q.4. a. New Jersey, Office of Economic Opportunity
       1966   Seasonal Farm Workers in New Jersey: A Report of the Migrant Opportunity Program. Trenton.
     b. vol. 7, p. 261

CHAPTER SEVEN

Q.2. a. 127:G1; 128:A11-13
     b. "Bill is Proposed to Close Adult Theaters"
Q.3. a. Study of marijuana smoking in Jamaica, commissioned by Natl Inst of Mental Health, fails to confirm any serious or adverse effects of marijuana use; . . .
     b. July 9, p. 21, column 1
Q.4. a. Steven J. Rosen
     b. Brandeis University

CHAPTER EIGHT

Q.2. a. Gaye Tuchman
     b. State University of New York at Stony Brook
     c. 1971 American Sociological Associated meetings
Q.3. a. "Classic on Classic: Parsons' Interpretation of Durkheim"
     b. Alpert, Harry
       1961   Emile Durkheim and His Sociology. New York: Russell & Russell.
Q.4. a. George L. Maddox
     b. Duke University
     c. pp. 668-69
Q.5. a. *British Humanities Index*
     b. p. 820

CHAPTER NINE

Q.2. *American Journal of Sociology*, 82:428-42, S '76. J. S. Coleman.
Q.3. a. Lee Ellis
     b. Minot State College
     c. pp. 307-08

CHAPTER TEN

Q.2. a. S181-44.1
     b. p. 707
     c. Donald W. Whitehead, Fed Co-chm, ARC
Q.3. a. (71) 7692
     b. "Sickness and Poverty, Handbook for Community Workers." 1970. 89 p.

CHAPTER ELEVEN

Q.2. a. 6224-2.3
     b. p. 162
Q.3. a. p. 99
     b. 73 p.

MATERIALS & METHODS FOR
SOCIOLOGY RESEARCH

Answers by Book

Book No. __17__

CHAPTER ONE
Q.2. a. *Dictionary of English Costume (900-1900)*
b. p. 395
Q.3. a. *Sociological Abstracts*
b. p. 263

CHAPTER TWO
Q.2. a. vol. 4, p. 323
b. Abel, Theodora M. and F. L. K. Hsu
1949 "Some aspects of personality of Chinese
as revealed by the Rorschach." Rorschach
Research Exchange 13:285-301.
Q.3. a. 6,951
b. p. 22
Q.4. a. 18.7%
b. 5.6%

CHAPTER THREE
Q.2. a. 2.31 per 1,000 population
b. p. 429
Q.3. a. 14.7 per 1,000 population
b. 41.8 per 1,000 population
c. p. 81
Q.4. a. 320.1
b. 217.4
c. pp. 157-58
Q.5. a. Phillip Bonacich. *Laboratory Experimentation in
Sociology.*
b. R. F. Bales
c. vol. 4, p. 145

CHAPTER FOUR
Q.2. a. *The Elementary Forms of the Religious Life*
b. vol. 9, p. 527
Q.3. a. W. G. Sumner
b. p. 79

CHAPTER FIVE
Q.3. a. Angle, J.
1976 "Mainland control of manufacturing and
reward for bilingualism in Puerto Rico."
American Sociological Review 41:289-307.
b. p. 284
Q.4. a. *Egypt: Population Problems and Prospects*
b. p. 47
Q.5. a. Robert M. Byrn. "Compulsory Lifesaving Treatment
for the Competent Adult"
b. p. 457
Q.6. a. "Organizing the Convicted: Self-help for Prisoners
and Ex-prisoners"
b. p. 221
Q.7. J. M. Fielding. "Problems of Evaluative Research
Group Into Psychotherapy Outcome"

CHAPTER SIX
Q.2. a. Michael Joseph Goldstein and others. *Pornography
and Sexual Deviance: A Rpt. of Legal
Behavioral Inst., Beverly Hills, California.*
b. p. 380

Q.3. a. R. E. Dawson. "Political Socialization"
b. p. 171
Q.4. a. Barnett, James Harwood
1968 Divorce and the American Divorce
1939 Novel, 1858-1937: A Study in Literary
Reflections of Social Influences.
New York: Russell & Russell.
b. vol. 11, p. 429

CHAPTER SEVEN
Q.2. a. 48:A4; 138:F5-6
b. "Porno Case of U. S. Nearly Complete"
Q.3. a. Charles Schmid Jr, convicted of killing 3 teen-age
girls in '60s, dies of stab wounds inflicted by other
inmates at Ariz State Prison (S)
b. March 31, p. 28, column 4
Q.4. a. Martin Glaberman
b. Wayne State, Wayne County Community College
and University of Detroit

CHAPTER EIGHT
Q.2. a. Robert K. Merton
b. Columbia University
c. November 6, 1969 to the seminar celebrating the
50th anniversary of the department of sociology
at the University of Bombay, India
Q.3. a. "Group Disorders in the Public Schools"
b. Bailey, Stephen K.
1970 Disruption in Urban Public Secondary
Schools. Washington: National Association
of Secondary School Principals.
Q.4. a. Stephen Schafer
b. Northeastern University
c. pp. 123-24
Q.5. a. *Historical Abstracts*
b. p. 820

CHAPTER NINE
Q.2. *Sociological Review,* ns 24:636-7, Ag '76.
I. M. L. Hunter.
Q.3. a. A. J. Bergesen
b. University of Arizona
c. p. 310

CHAPTER TEN
Q.2. a. S181-40.17
b. p. 510
c. Arthur S. Flemming, Chm, Commission on
Civil Rights
Q.3. a. (70) 1333
b. "Socioeconomic Trends in Poverty Areas, 1960-68."
1969. 21 p.

CHAPTER ELEVEN
Q.2. a. 4564-4
b. p. 146
Q.3. a. p. 96
b. 99 p.

MATERIALS & METHODS FOR
SOCIOLOGY RESEARCH

Answers by Book

Book No. __18__

CHAPTER ONE

Q.2. a. *Current Clinical Dental Terminology, A Glossary of Accepted Terms in All Disciplines of Dentistry*
b. p. 814
Q.3. a. *Abstracts for Social Workers*
b. p. 264

CHAPTER TWO

Q.2. a. vol. 4, p. 418
b. Aberle, D. F.
1951 "The Psychosocial Analysis of a Hopi Life-history." Comparative Psychology Monographs 21:no. 2.
Q.3. a. 8,983
b. p. 22
Q.4. a. 35.5%
b. 4.6%

CHAPTER THREE

Q.2. a. 0.41 per 1,000 population
b. p. 429
Q.3. a. 14.7 per 1,000 population
b. 49.6 per 1,000 population
c. p. 83
Q.4. a. 328.2
b. 217.6
c. pp. 157-58
Q.5. a. N. J. Demerath III and W. C. Roof. *Religion—Recent Strands in Research.*
b. H. Abramson
c. vol. 2, p. 19

CHAPTER FOUR

Q.2. a. *Historical Materialism: A System of Sociology*
b. vol. 10, p. 52
Q.3. a. Max Weber
b. p. 94

CHAPTER FIVE

Q.3. a. Janovitz, B. S.
1976 "Analysis of the impact of education on family size." Demography 13:189-98.
b. p. 317
Q.4. a. "A Population Dynamics Survey in Lagos, Nigeria"
b. p. 47
Q.5. a. Peter Bernholz. "Is a Paretian Liberal Really Impossible"
b. p. 762
Q.6. a. "Federal Prison Industry—The Green Monster: Part One—History and Background"
b. p. 159
Q.7. D. E. Harrison, W. H. Bennett, G. Globetti and M. Alsikafi. "Premarital Sexual Stand of Rural Youth"

CHAPTER SIX

Q.2. a. Alan R. Coffey. *Juvenile Justice as a System: Law Enforcement to Rehabilitation.*
b. p. 226

Q.3. a. J. W. Soule. "Future Political Ambitions and the Behavior of Incumbent State Legislators"
b. p. 103
Q.4. a. Hippchen, Leonard Joseph
1966 Personnel and Personnel Practices in Public Institutions for Delinquent Children: A Survey. Washington: U. S. Dept. of Health, Education, and Welfare, Welfare Administration, Children's Bureau.
b. vol. 22, p. 357

CHAPTER SEVEN

Q.2. a. 72:G2; 110:F5-6
b. "Operators Warned"
Q.3. a. 8-yr-old Colo welfare recipient Franci O'Donnells' comments to panel of Cabinet officers and Domestic Council staff members during 1st in series of White House public forums on domestic policy noted; . . .
b. October 22, p. 23, column 1
Q.4. a. Natalie Allon
b. Hofstra University

CHAPTER EIGHT

Q.2. a. Herbert J. Gans
b. Columbia University and Center for Policy Research
c. Vassar College conference on the war on poverty in 1964, at the 7th World Congress of Sociology in 1971, and in *Social Policy* 2 (July-August 1971): 20-24.
Q.3. a. "Some Developmental Interpersonal Dynamics Through Childhood"
b. Bales, R. F.
1950 Interaction Process Analysis. Cambridge, Massachusetts: Addison-Wesley.
Q.4. a. Gay C. Kitson
b. Case Western Reserve University
c. pp. 118-19
Q.5. a. *Psychological Abstracts*
b. p. 820

CHAPTER NINE

Q.2. *American Journal of Sociology,* 82:747-8, N '76. M. N. Zald.
Q.3. a. George A. Kourvetaris
b. Northern Illinois University
c. pp. 328-29

CHAPTER TEN

Q.2. a. H181-53.2
b. p. 73
c. William S. Whitehead, Chm, Renegotiation Bd.
Q.3. a. (65) 8358
b. "Attack on Poverty." 1965. pp. 9-12.

CHAPTER ELEVEN

Q.2. a. 6064-12
b. p. 13
Q.3. a. p. 97
b. 72 p.

MATERIALS & METHODS FOR
SOCIOLOGY RESEARCH

Answers by Book

Book No. ___19___

CHAPTER ONE

Q.2. a. *Electronics and Nucleonics Dictionary*
b. p. 788
Q.3. a. *International Bibliography of Sociology*
b. p. 266

CHAPTER TWO

Q.2. a. vol. 4, p. 507
b. Abel, T.
1938 Why Hitler Came to Power.
New York: Prentice-Hall.
Q.3. a. 11,133
b. p. 22
Q.4. a. 23.6%
b. 4.9%

CHAPTER THREE

Q.2. a. 1.69 per 1,000 population
b. p. 429
Q.3. a. 14.7 per 1,000 population
b. 49.2 per 1,000 population
c. p. 81
Q.4. a. 847.0
b. 314.7
c. pp. 157-58
Q.5. a. Samuel H. Preston. *Mortality Trends.*
b. G. Acsádi and J. Nemeskéri
c. vol. 3, p. 163

CHAPTER FOUR

Q.2. a. *The Origins of Totalitarianism*
b. vol. 10, p. 64
Q.3. a. Destutt de Tracy
b. p. 94

CHAPTER FIVE

Q.3. a. Berry, J. S. and R. O. Hansson
1976 "Birth order and institutionalization of
the aged." Journal of Social Psychology
99:295-96.
b. p. 14
Q.4. a. *Education, Income Distribution and Rate of Urban
Migration in Tanzania*
b. p. 99
Q.5. a. Ulla Olin. "Controls in Animal and Human
Populations"
b. p. 866
Q.6. a. *The States Combat White Collar Crime*
b. p. 143
Q.7. W. Ketcham, A. Sack, and H. Shore. "Annotated
Bibliography on Alternatives to Institutional Care"

CHAPTER SIX

Q.2. a. Gerald Vivian Stimson. *Heroin and Behaviour:
Diversity Among Addicts Attending London Clinics.*
b. p. 285
Q.3. a. R. E. Kanet. "The Rise and Fall of the 'All-People's
State': Recent Changes in the Soviet Theory of
the State"
b. p. 139
Q.4. a. Ackerley, Joe Randolph
1968 My Father & Myself. London: Bodley Head.
b. vol. 19, p. 281

CHAPTER SEVEN

Q.2. a. 13:E14; 1:F1
b. "Mining Museum Tops List for Bicentennial Project"
Q.3. a. Pope restates opposition to divorce, message to Natl
Conf of Cath Bishops
b. January 5, p. 2, column 5
Q.4. a. David Mechanic
b. University of Wisconsin

CHAPTER EIGHT

Q.2. a. Edward A. Tiryakian
b. Duke University
c. 1971 meetings of the American Sociological
Association
Q.3. a. "A Theory of Middleman Minorities"
b. Basil, Anne
1969 Armenian Settlements in India.
West Bengal: Armenian College.
Q.4. a. Leland J. Axelson
b. Florida State University
c. pp. 243-44
Q.5. a. *Abstracts for Social Workers*
b. p. 813

CHAPTER NINE

Q.2. *Sociological Review,* ns 23:924-5, N '75. C. Brookes.
Q.3. a. S. D. Berkowitz
b. University of Toronto
c. pp. 428-30

CHAPTER TEN

Q.2. a. H761-4.3
b. p. 385
c. James Abdnor, Rep, R-S Dak
Q.3. a. (64) 12533
b. "Women's Role in War on Poverty." 1964. 8 p.

CHAPTER ELEVEN

Q.2. a. 4824-15
b. p. 7
Q.3. a. p. 98
b. 6 p.

MATERIALS & METHODS FOR
SOCIOLOGY RESEARCH

Answers by Book

Book No. __20__

CHAPTER ONE

Q.2. a. *Technical Dictionary of Data Processing, Computers, Office Machines*
b. p. 790
Q.3. a. *Bibliographic Survey: The Negro in Print*
b. p. 267

CHAPTER TWO

Q.2. a. vol. 4, p. 611
b. Allee, W. C.
1931 Animal Aggregations. Chicago: University of Chicago Press.
Q.3. a. 12,288
b. p. 22
Q.4. a. 24.7%
b. 6.0%

CHAPTER THREE

Q.2. a. 1.41 per 1,000 population
b. p. 429
Q.3. a. 14.7 per 1,000 population
b. 42.9 per 1,000 population
c. p. 81
Q.4. a. 403.5
b. 148.7
c. pp. 157-58
Q.5. a. Charles C. Moskos, Jr. *The Military.*
b. B. Abrahamsson
c. vol. 2, p. 55

CHAPTER FOUR

Q.2. a. *The Nature of Prejudice*
b. vol. 10, p. 370
Q.3. a. Clarence Perry
b. p. 124

CHAPTER FIVE

Q.3. a. Cutright, P. and P. Madras
1976 "A.F.D.C. and the marital and family status of ever married women aged 15-44: United States 1950-1970." Sociology and Social Research 60:314-27.
b. p. 565
Q.4. a. *Essays on the Population of Taiwan*
b. p. 275
Q.5. a. David L. Paletz and William F. Harris. "Four-letter Threats to Authority"
b. p. 772
Q.6. a. "Dimensions of the Dark Figure of Unreported Crime"
b. p. 198
Q.7. R. M. Grinnell and N. S. Kyte. "Modifying Environment"

CHAPTER SIX

Q.2. a. Joel Fort. *Alcohol: Our Biggest Drug Problem.*
b. p. 13

Q.3. a. O. Ruin. "Patterns of Government Composition in Multi-party Systems: The Case of Sweden"
b. p. 147
Q.4. a. Cromwell, Rue L.
1967 The Development of Behavior Dimensions for Emotionally Disturbed Children: A Study of Relevant Indicators for Classroom Techniques, Therapeutic Methods, and Prognosis. Nashville: Vanderbilt University.
b. vol. 26, p. 245

CHAPTER SEVEN

Q.2. a. 5:C2; 8:E2-3
b. "Idaho Bicentennial Planning Termed Best in West"
Q.3. a. SIC, after 1-½-yr study of NYS jails, urges end to continual arrests of chronic alcoholics; . . .
b. January 1, p. 36, column 2
Q.4. a. Howard S. Becker
b. Northwestern University

CHAPTER EIGHT

Q.2. a. Harvey A. Kantor
b. University of Rhode Island
c. Fourth Annual Meeting of Cheiron: International Society for the History of the Social and Behavioral Sciences, University of Calgary, Alberta, Canada, June 30, 1972.
Q.3. a. "Values and Violence: A Test of the Subculture of Violence Thesis"
b. Baker, R. and S. Ball
1969 Violence and the Media. Washington, D. C.: U. S. G. P. O.
Q.4. a. J. Kenneth Benson
b. University of Missouri, Columbia
c. p. 378
Q.5. a. *Public Affairs Information Service*
b. p. 814

CHAPTER NINE

Q.2. *Sociological Review,* ns 24:157-9, F '76. D. Fraser.
Q.3. a. Craig Calhoun
b. St. Antony's College Oxford University
c. pp. 447-48

CHAPTER TEN

Q.2. a. H181-67.8
b. p. 87
c. Gloria E. A. Toote, Asst Sec, Equal Opportunity
Q.3. a. (64) 16927
b. "Women in Poverty." 1964. 7 leaves.

CHAPTER ELEVEN

Q.2. a. 104-1.2
b. pp. 171-86
Q.3. a. pp. 16-17
b. 265 p.

Materials & Methods
for
Sociology Research
Workbook

TABLE OF CONTENTS

ACKNOWLEDGEMENTS

The technique of using a manual to teach bibliographic skills was first developed by Miriam Dudley of UCLA. There is no more apt beginning for those who build upon the method than to acknowledge her work. In deciding upon the materials to include in this manual, the classification of them, and the sorts of things to say about them, the authors have benefited from close consideration of Sources of Information in the Social Sciences edited by Carl White, Literature and Bibliography of the Social Sciences by Thelma Freides, and Social Science Research Handbook by Raymond G. McInnis and James W. Scott. The flow charts in Chapter Twelve were redrawn and modified from Thomas Kirk, "Problems in Library Instruction in Four-Year Colleges" in Educating the Library User (New York: R. R. Bowker) edited by John Lubans, pages 93-95.

The development of a teaching source such as this manual requires the efforts of many people. First, the authors are greatly indebted to Carla J. Stoffle, series editor, for her guidance and encouragement throughout the writing of the material. A special thanks is given to Charles A. Goldsmid for reviewing an early draft of the manual and providing many useful suggestions, and to Gail Kummings for editing a revised draft. For their assistance in the preparation of this manual, the authors are grateful to several members of the University of Wisconsin-Parkside's Library/Learning Center Staff. Among them, Julie Richter and Shirley Mandernack deserve special thanks. The authors are also indebted to the University of Wisconsin System for the 1977/78 Undergraduate Teaching Improvement Grant and to the Council on Library Resources and National Endowment to the Humanities for the College Library Program Grant which provided resources to make the development of this manual possible. Finally, the students of three successive years in the sociology methods course at UW-Parkside deserve acknowledgement. Each year the classes absorbed the material and tested the exercises. Their reactions in turn served as indicators for extensive revisions of the manual.

INTRODUCTION

The ability to locate information in an organized and efficient manner is an important asset for students. The more they know about the materials and methods necessary for effective information gathering, the more productive and less time consuming will they find their research and independent study time. In addition, effective library research skills will enable students after they leave school to further their educational development through the use of information sources available at most libraries.

This manual focuses on methods of information gathering and types of information sources appropriate for research and independent study in sociology. The specific objectives of the manual are: to introduce basic types of information sources that sociology students should be able to use, to familiarize students with important examples of each type of source, and to prepare students to use those information sources efficiently and effectively in independent study and research. Upon completion of the assignments in this manual, students should be able to:

--identify and use content reference works in sociology
   (dictionaries, encyclopedias, handbooks, and yearbooks);

--identify and use specialized finding aids (bibliographies, guides, and indexes);

--locate and use government publications, especially

Bureau of the Census material;

--locate articles in sociology journals, newspapers,
and general periodicals;

--evaluate the quality of a book or article by using
reviews or the criteria discussed in the workbook;

--utilize specific research techniques and search
strategies for efficient and effective information
gathering;

--cite periodicals, books, and documents according to
standard bibliographic form.

To place the above objectives in the context of a specific example, suppose you have been assigned a paper or want
information on Juvenile Delinquency. With the materials
introduced and explained in the workbook, you should be able
to find quickly and easily: a concise definition of "juvenile
delinquency"; lists of articles and books written about the
topic; discussions of different theories about the causes of
juvenile delinquency and the impact it has upon American
society; reviews of books to help you select a balanced coverage; and government statistics about the frequency of juvenile
delinquency according to age, geographic region, race, and
social class background.

This manual is divided into twelve chapters and an
appendix. In each of the first eleven chapters a category or
type of bibliographic tool is described; then, examples of
that type are introduced and assignments designed to teach its
use follow. The chapters are arranged so that the student will

become familiar first with the nature and uses of inclusive
reference works, then with the nature and uses of specialized
studies (articles or book-length treatments of a single
sociological topic), and finally with examples of the descriptive data (in particular government statistics) that the
professional sociologist uses. The last chapter discusses
techniques and strategies which place the skills learned
earlier into a research context. At the end of the workbook
there is an appendix containing additional examples of the
types of sources discussed in each chapter.

In each of the chapters of this manual, the organization
of the sources under discussion and their utility for sociology
students is explained, then standard examples of the type are
described individually. In the assignments accompanying the
chapters, students are asked to use those standard sources to
locate information. Each brief assignment translates the
discussion in a chapter to practical experience demonstrating
the ease with which sources can be located and information
secured.

The intention behind this manual is not to present an
exhaustive treatment of its subject matter. Rather, the
bibliographic examples have been selected according to the
following criteria: they are all in the English language,
they are generally available in medium size college libraries,
and they are important examples of the types of sources most
useful to sociology students.

Too often, learning bibliographic skills is an unnecessarily haphazard and time consuming process that leaves students unfamiliar with many types of sources that would increase the ease and productivity of their study hours. It is hoped that this manual will offer those who use it a more thorough and less frustrating introduction to bibliographic sources useful to the study of sociology than was heretofore available.

NOTE TO THE STUDENT

In order to carry out research efficiently, you must be
familiar with the library's major services and collections,
its classification system for books and periodicals, and the
arrangement of the card catalogue. If you have questions
about these matters consult either the printed descriptive
materials available in the library or a reference librarian
before you begin to use this manual.

A few simple procedures, if followed as you use this
manual, will maximize its benefits to you and minimize the
time you spend on the exercises. Be sure to read the text
material, and especially the source annotations, carefully
before turning to the assignment sheet for each chapter. Read
the entire assignment sheet before attempting to do any of the
questions, and make a preliminary decision about which source
discussed in the chapter is appropriate for each question.
When using a source for the first time, examine its table of
contents, explanatory material in its preface and/or introduction, and the index, if there is one, to determine how the
source can most efficiently be used.

There are no "trick" questions in the assignments. If
you spend more than ten to fifteen minutes on an individual
question, your approach to the problem may be incorrect. Ask
a reference librarian for advice. You should also seek help
from a reference librarian when you cannot find a source

where it should be shelved or on a nearby table in the reference area.

Finally, because each of the chapters in this manual has a very specific focus, it is important to read the Introduction carefully. Beside imparting an initial sense of the content of the manual, it should convey an idea of the overall research ability to which each of the chapters contributes.

Chapter 1

GUIDES TO THE LITERATURE

Objective 1:   After reading this chapter, the student will
               describe a situation in which a guide would
               be useful.
Objective 2:   Given a subject field other than a social or
               behavioral science, the student will use
               Guide to Reference Books to identify an appro-
               priate example of a specified type of reference
               source (a guide, encyclopedia, bibliography,
               etc.).
Objective 3:   Given a topic in sociology, the student will
               use Sources of Information in the Social Sciences
               to identify a specified reference work.

    Guides to the literature introduce the various types of

publications available in a given subject field or fields.

The purpose of a guide is to identify the sources that will

enable students to successfully undertake information searches

on an individual topic. There are guides which focus nearly

exclusively on the two principal categories of reference works:

finding aids, such as bibliographies and periodical indexes;

and content reference works, such as handbooks, subject dic-

tionaries, and subject encyclopedias. In addition to reference

works, some guides include discussions of various types of

research materials, such as government publications, while

others include lists of important book-length studies on topics

in a subject field.

    Students who are unfamiliar with a particular subject

discipline can identify its reference publications by consulting

a guide which attempts to cover a wide spectrum of the fields of knowledge. The standard general guide is:

Sheehy, Eugene P. Guide to Reference Books. 9th ed.
Chicago: American Library Association, 1976.

     The primary purpose of this volume is to list and
evaluate reference sources. Individual books are grouped
under these headings: General Reference Works, Humanities,
Social Sciences, History and Area Studies, Pure and
Applied Sciences. Within each group, titles are subdivided
by subject, then by specific type of material (encyclopedia,
dictionary, bibliography, etc.). The ninth edition lists
over 10,500 titles, most of which were published before
1973, although some 1974 reference works are included.
There is an index to authors, titles, and specific topics.

For most academic disciplines there are specialized guides

to the literature. Given an unfamiliar topic in sociology or

a related field, a student can consult a guide which focuses

on the social sciences for titles of content reference works

containing information on the topic and of finding aids iden-

tifying scholarly books and articles on it. The best example

is:

White, Carl. Sources of Information in the Social Sciences.
2nd ed. Chicago: American Library Association, 1973.

     This one-volume guide covers eight social sciences,
each in a separate chapter. The first part of each
chapter introduces important monographs on the development, organization, and content of a discipline and its
subfields; the second part lists and annotates major
reference works in the discipline by type (dictionaries,
encyclopedias, handbooks, etc.). There is an inclusive
author-title-subject index.

Chapter 1

GUIDES TO THE LITERATURE

Assignment

1. Describe a situation in which you as a sociology student
    would use a guide to the literature. Be specific.

2. You are taking _____

    _____
    and the instructor has asked each student to select an
    independent study project. In defining your project you
    feel you should consult specialized reference sources in
    the subject field. To identify these, you consult
    Guide to Reference Books.

    a. What is the title of the first English language
        dictionary listed for your subject field?

    b. On what page did you find this information?

3. Your instructor is conducting your sociological research
    methods course in the library for several class periods
    in order to familiarize the students with basic reference
    sources. To involve the class actively, he has asked
    each student to be ready to explain how a particular
    type of reference source can be used in sociological
    research and to use an individual title as an example of
    the type. You have been asked to identify _____

    _____.
    For individual titles you consult Sources of Information
    in the Social Sciences.

a. What is the title of the first English language publication which meets your requirements?

b. On which page(s) is that title discussed?

Chapter 2

HANDBOOKS

Objective 1:   After reading this chapter, the student will
                describe a situation in which a sociologist
                would use a handbook.
Objective 2:   Using the Handbook of Social Psychology, the
                student will locate specific information about
                a topic or theoretical approach discussed by
                sociologists.
Objective 3:   Given Historical Statistics of the United States,
                the student will locate statistics on a specified
                demographic characteristic.
Objective 4:   Given County and City Data Book, the student will
                locate comparative statistics for two counties.

A handbook is a compact fact book designed for quick
reference. Usually a handbook deals with one broad subject
area, and emphasizes generally accepted data rather than recent
findings. In the latter respect handbooks differ from yearbooks, discussed in Chapter Three, although these reference
tools overlap in the way they are used and the information
they include. Two types of handbooks useful to sociologists
are: statistical handbooks, which provide data about a number
of demographic and social characteristics, and subject handbooks, which offer a comprehensive summary of research findings
and theoretical propositions for broad substantive areas in a
discipline.

Containing data gathered from several different sources,
statistical handbooks provide students with information necessary for the description and analysis of social trends and
phenomena in a convenient and reliable form. Among the

statistical handbooks useful to sociologists are:

> U. S. Bureau of the Census. <u>County and City Data Book</u>. Washington, D. C.: Government Printing Office, 1949-.
>
> This handbook contains statistics on population, housing, income, education, and employment for counties, standard metropolitan statistical areas, cities, urbanized areas, and unincorporated places. Since there is no subject index, the only subject access to the tables is through the "Outline of Tabular Subject Content" located in the front of the volume. This handbook is published irregularly.
>
> <u>Historical Statistics of the United States: Colonial Times to 1970</u>. Washington, D. C.: Government Printing Office, 1975.
>
> This two-volume work contains statistics on a wide spectrum of social and economic developments from the colonial period to the present. The tables are accompanied by explanatory notes and references to additional sources of statistical information. To use this work effectively, the student may turn to the table of contents, which provides a broad subject access; the subject index, which offers a more narrow topical approach to the data; or the time period index, which provides access to statistics on major topics for individual decades.

Subject handbooks in sociology provide a summary and a synthesis of concepts, research, and theoretical approaches of specific topical areas within the discipline (e.g., formal organizations, socialization, and social psychology). Students who want a brief overview of well established information or an explanation of major concepts in one substantive area, such as social psychology, will find that the subject handbook listed below is a convenient source:

> Lindzey, Gardner and Elliot Aronson, eds. <u>Handbook of Social Psychology</u>. 2nd ed. Reading, Mass.: Addison-Wesley, 1968-69. 5 vols.
>
> Divided into five volumes, this handbook contains chapters covering major aspects of social psychology,

e.g., systematic positions, research methods, the
individual in a social context, group psychology and
group interaction, and applied social psychology.
Chapters are written by professionals in the field of
social psychology and range from 50 to 100 pages in
length, followed by bibliographies which are useful
although somewhat dated. Author and subject indexes
provide access to each volume; volume five contains
cumulative author and subject indexes for the complete
set.

Chapter 2

HANDBOOKS

Assignment

1. Describe a situation in which a sociology student would
    use a handbook.

2. You have just covered the topic _____
    _____ in your social psychology
    class, and you want to do some extra readings on the topic
    before the exam. Because you are pressed for time, you
    want a concise statement about the topic, as well as a
    few suggestions for further reading.

    a. Using the Handbook of Social Psychology, in what
        volume and on what page will you find an essay that
        covers this topic?

    b. What is the complete citation for the first English
        language publication in the bibliography? (See
        Chapter Twelve, page 72 for examples of complete
        citations.)

3. A topic discussed by your demography instructor is the
    pattern of population growth of the United States during
    the first 100 years of its existence. She assigns each
    student in the class a geographical area and a year. You
    have been asked to locate the population figure in the
    Historical Statistics of the United States for the _____
    _____ region in _____.

a. What is the total population for this region?

b. On what page did you find this information?

4. In your social problems course, the class has been asked
    to test the hypothesis that poverty in urban areas is
    more severe than poverty in rural areas. Using the 1977
    edition of County and City Data Book, find the percentage
    of families with incomes below poverty level in a southern
    rural county and in a northeastern urban county.

    a. What is the percentage of people with incomes below
        poverty level in _____?

    b. What is the percentage of people with incomes below
        poverty level in _____?

Chapter 3

YEARBOOKS

Objective 1:   After reading this chapter, the student will
               describe a situation in which a yearbook would
               be an appropriate source of information.
Objective 2:   Using Demographic Yearbook, the student will
               determine the divorce rate for a given country.
Objective 3:   Using the Statistical Yearbook, the student will
               compare the birth rate of a specific country to
               that of the United States.
Objective 4:   Using Uniform Crime Reports, the student will
               locate the crime rate for a specific size city in
               the United States.
Objective 5:   Using Annual Review of Sociology, the student will
               identify current research on a given topic.

While in many cases they contain a good deal of background

information, yearbooks are fact books which focus on the

developments and events of a given year. Unlike the handbooks

discussed in the preceding chapter, they emphasize current

information. Like handbooks, there are two types of yearbooks

most useful for sociology students: statistical yearbooks,

which provide the most recent data on social and demographic

characteristics, and subject yearbooks, which review current

theory and research.

Although sociology students will frequently turn to the

most recent yearbook for the latest data available on topics

such as population composition, fertility, and economic

activity, they will also need to use back issues to collect

data for previous time periods. This is especially true in

cases where no handbook presents data for a specific geographical

or topical area. Among the general statistical yearbooks most frequently used by sociologists is:

United Nations. Statistical Office. <u>Statistical</u>
<u>Yearbook</u>. New York: 1949-.

 This annual publication is prepared by the Statistical Office of the United Nations. Tables cover
population, manpower, agriculture, production, mining
construction, consumption, transportation, external
trade, wages and prices, national income, finance,
social statistics, education and culture. Normally, a
10-20 year span is given for each series. The table of
contents is the only subject access to this book. Sources
are cited. Textual material, including indexes, is in
French and English.

Statistical yearbooks focusing on a special subject are

often useful to sociologists interested in specific problems.

Two yearbooks focusing on specific subjects are:

United Nations. Statistical Office. <u>Demographic</u>
<u>Yearbook</u>. New York: 1948-.

 This annual contains demographic statistics for
over 200 separate geographic areas. Population and vital
statistics appear in each annual volume, but the subject
matter of the other statistical compilations varies from
year to year. An introduction defining terms and
describing the tables is included in each volume. Access
to tables by broad category is provided in the table of
contents. A cumulative index in each volume identifies
the annual volumes in which statistics on individual
topics are to be found, and indicates the time span of
the statistics in individual volumes.

U. S. Federal Bureau of Investigation. <u>Uniform Crime</u>
<u>Reports for the United States</u>. Washington, D. C.:
Government Printing Office, 1930-.

 This annual report contains statistics on crimes,
offenders, and law enforcement personnel. Tables include
statistics by type of offenses, geographical divisions,
age groups, trends, and police employment. The table of
contents provides the only subject access to the tables.

The subject yearbook (also known as the annual review)

is particularly useful because it contains articles which give a brief overview of recent major developments in the field. These articles, based on the latest published research, can be used by a student beginning a research project to define and clarify the subject matter. In addition, the bibliographies appended to the articles can provide useful leads for further reading. The subject yearbook for sociology is:

Annual Review of Sociology. Palo Alto, Calif.: Annual Reviews, 1975-.

    New developments in the field of sociology are discussed in approximately 16 essays covering ten broad subject areas in this annual. Areas covered include formal organizations, social processes, urban sociology, and institutions. The essays average 25-30 pages in length and include extensive bibliographies. Each volume, beginning with the second, contains cumulative indexes which list essays by author and broad subject area.

Chapter 3

YEARBOOKS

Assignment

1. Describe a situation in which a sociology student would use a yearbook.

2. An interesting issue has been raised in your sociology of the family course concerning modernization and family instability. You decide to see if there is a relationship between increased modernization and increased family instability by comparing the divorce rates of a variety of countries at different stages of development. Using the Demographic Yearbook for 1975, you search for the divorce rates of 10 countries, one of which is _____
   _____.

   a. What is the 1974 divorce rate for your country?

   b. On what page did you find this information?

3. In her lectures, your sociology instructor has talked about the population crisis in the world. She asserts that this crisis is much more severe in underdeveloped nations. To test this assertion, you have been asked to compare the crude birth rate of _____ to that of the United States using the Statistical Yearbook, 1976.

   a. What is the crude birth rate of the United States?

b.　What is the crude birth rate of the country given?

c.　On what page did you find this information?

4.　Your sociology of crime and delinquency class has been discussing the effect of urbanization on crime rates and the theory that crime rates are higher for large urban areas than for small towns.　To test this assertion, your class has broken into groups to gather data on various offenses.　Your group is researching _____ _____.　You turn to Uniform Crime Reports for the United States to find the crime rates for a breakdown of offenses known to police in 1977.

a.　What is the <u>rate</u> per 100,000 inhabitants for cities of _____ population?

b.　What is the <u>rate</u> per 100,000 inhabitants for cities of _____ population?

c.　On what page(s) did you find this answer?

5.　You have covered a number of topics in your sociology theory course.　The instructor has asked you to summarize the current state of theory and research in (on) _____ _____ _____.

a. Using the cumulative index in the 1978 _Annual Review of Sociology_, cite the author and title of such a summary.

b. Who is the author of the first book-length treatment of the topic presented in the bibliography?

c. In what volume and on what page is this summary located?

Chapter 4

SUBJECT DICTIONARIES AND ENCYCLOPEDIAS

Objective 1: After reading this chapter, the student will describe a situation in which a subject dictionary or subject encyclopedia would be useful in sociological research or study.

Objective 2: Given a term or concept in sociology, the student will use Dictionary of Sociology to determine the original source of the term or concept.

Objective 3: Given a research topic in sociology, the student will locate an essay in International Encyclopedia of the Social Sciences which provides background information on that topic, and will identify the first item in the bibliography which accompanies the essay.

The primary purpose of a dictionary is to indicate the meanings of words. The words included, and the exhaustiveness of their definitions, depend upon the type of dictionary. There are basically four types of dictionaries: those which are of a general nature (abridged and unabridged); those which focus on specific aspects of language (synonyms, slang, etymology); those which translate words from one language to another; and those which concentrate on individual subject areas. This discussion focuses on the fourth type, subject dictionaries.

Virtually all academic disciplines have their own specialized "language." The function of a subject dictionary is to explain briefly the words, whether terms or names, that make up a particular subject's specialized jargon. Such a source lists terms unfamiliar in common usage, as well as rather ordinary terms that have taken on specialized and technical meanings within the context of a subject discipline.

Sociology is a broad field encompassing virtually every aspect of human social behavior. Many concepts or terms that have a common usage, or that apply to a specific aspect of social life, take on a specialized meaning in sociology. The term "norm" is an example. In common usage the word refers to something common or "normal." Within sociology, however, "norm" refers to the rules or sets of expectations that guide social behavior. In addition to defining concepts, subject dictionaries in sociology are also useful for locating brief descriptions of methodological techniques or tests and definitions of major theories. Therefore, if students are unsure either of the exact meaning of a concept or theory or of the function of a specific methodological technique, they should consult a sociology dictionary. A dictionary used by sociologists is:

Mitchell, G. Duncan. _Dictionary of Sociology_. Chicago: Aldine, 1968.

This comprehensive dictionary, prepared for the student sociologist, contains extensive definitions of words as they are used by sociologists. Definitions for each term include historical usage, origin of the term, and references to other sources of information on the topic. Definitions vary in length from a few lines to two or three pages.

While dictionaries contain brief definitions of terms, encyclopedias contain summary essays about individual topics. There are two types of encyclopedias: general encyclopedias, which are wide-ranging in topical coverage, and subject encyclopedias, which focus on topics within an individual subject discipline or a group of related disciplines. The rest of this discussion will deal with subject encyclopedias.

The essays in subject encyclopedias are written by recognized scholars. They are accompanied by bibliographies listing major studies of the topic and by cross references listing other essays in the encyclopedia which may contain useful additional information. Students can therefore profitably use an essay in a subject encyclopedia in several ways--as an initial introduction to a topic about which they know very little, as a means of rounding out and placing a topic in a wider context, or as the starting point for research they intend to do on an aspect of a topic. The student engaged in research may find an essay on the topic useful for clarification and definition of the research project, and the bibliography accompanying the essay can provide valuable leads for further reading.

The subject encyclopedia that is especially useful to sociology majors is:

International Encyclopedia of the Social Sciences. New York: Macmillan, 1968. 17 vols.

This 17-volume set contains articles covering the subject matter of--and some of the most important contributors in the development of--anthropology, economics, geography, history, law, political science, psychiatry, psychology, sociology, and statistics. The treatment of individual topics is often divided into more than one essay, each approaching the topic from the perspective of a different social science. Although the encyclopedia is arranged alphabetically by subject, the articles are lengthy and cover broad areas. In order to find a specific topic, the index in the last volume should always be consulted. There is also a useful "Classification of Articles" section in the last volume. The essays themselves are carefully cross-referenced, and the bibliographies accompanying the articles, some of which are extensive although dated, remain useful.

Chapter 4

SUBJECT DICTIONARIES AND ENCYCLOPEDIAS

Assignment

1. Describe a situation in which a sociology student would use a subject dictionary or encyclopedia.

2. You are assigned a term paper in your contemporary American society class on the topic _____ _____. You would like a general introduction to the topic and books or articles on it.

   a. Using Internatonal Encyclopedia of the Social Sciences, what is the title of the first English language book in the bibliography of the essay on this topic?

   b. In what volume and on what page did you find this information?

3. You are familiar with the meaning of the term _____ _____ but you are not sure of its source. Since you are writing a paper in which you use the term, you want to be sure to credit the person who originated it.

   a. Using Dictionary of Sociology, who first used the term?

   b. On what page did you find this information?

Chapter 5

ABSTRACTS AND INDEXES

Objective 1:   After reading this chapter, the student will
                describe a situation in which indexes and
                abstracts are useful and will identify the basic
                differences between the two.
Objective 2:   The student will use the indexes listed in this
                chapter to obtain citations for journal articles
                on specific topics.
Objective 3:   The student will use the abstracts listed in this
                chapter to obtain the citations for journal
                articles on specific topics.
Objective 4:   Given a topic and Social Sciences Citation Index
                listed in this chapter, the student will find an
                article related to an already identified earlier
                work.

Indexes and abstracts are used by researchers primarily

to identify journal articles on specific topics. Most indexes

and abstracts are published several times a year, with annual

cumulations. The Readers' Guide to Periodical Literature (see

Appendix for complete citation), listing general magazine

articles by subject (see Chapter Seven), is an index familiar

to most students; however, more specialized indexes and abstracts

list articles published in scholarly journals by subject and

author. The standard citation for articles in indexes includes

the author's name, the article title, the name of the journal,

the volume number and the date of the issue in which the article

appears, and the page numbers. For sociology students, indexes

and abstracts are important because the articles in scholarly

journals often update information found in books or in some

cases constitute the only published treatments of certain topics.

Sociologists need to be aware that some indexes identify articles in journals by the discipline or group of related disciplines (e.g., social sciences) rather than by the topic; others identify journal articles according to broad topical areas without a discipline focus. An example of the former, which indexes by subject articles in social science, economics, and anthropology journals as well as those in sociology is:

Social Sciences Index. New York: H. W. Wilson, 1974/75-.

     A quarterly publication with annual cumulations, this index organizes--by subject and author--articles in some 260 journals in anthropology, sociology, law, and criminology. A helpful feature is the separate "Book Reviews" index at the back of each issue.

Sometimes a topic is so important that it generates an index simply to make all relevant articles available to researchers, regardless of field or discipline. An example of such an index which is frequently used by sociologists is:

Population Index. Princeton, N. J.: Office of Population Research, Princeton University and Population Association of America, 1935-.

     Books, journals, and government publications are indexed in this quarterly. The annotated entries are arranged by broad subjects, such as mortality, internal migration, and spatial distribution. Each issue also contains several articles on topics of current interest. Geographical, author, and statistical indexes cumulate annually.

The third type of index employed by sociologists is a relatively new finding aid. The "Citation Index" identifies articles which have referred to previous research by a particular author. When a researcher knows of one article--or author of

articles--on a particular topic, newer related materials can
be found by locating articles which cite the original work
or author. An advantage of this type of index is that a
researcher can find articles without depending on any subject
classification system. A disadvantage, however, is that this
type of indexing does not clearly distinguish the relationship
of the later articles to the cited work. These citations must
then be located to determine their usefulness. This type of
index is useful for determining the quality of a specific key
research paper, or for tracing the developments in theory and
methods which were stimulated by this key paper. A student
can determine the number of times a key article has been used,
as well as the names of the sociologists who have cited it.
The citation index useful to sociologists is:

> Social Sciences Citation Index. Philadelphia: Institute
> for Scientific Information, 1972-.
>
> This service enables the user to identify recent
> articles that refer to earlier works. Each issue is
> divided into three parts. The Citation Index, arranged
> alphabetically by cited author, lists references to
> articles in which a particular work was cited. The Source
> Index lists the authors who are citing the original work
> alphabetically and gives bibliographic information for
> each article which cites the original work. The Permaterm
> Subject Index lists articles by all the significant words
> in the titles. The index is issued three times a year and
> cumulates annually.

Like indexes, abstracts provide a complete citation for
each article. They also include a brief summary of its contents.
This summary, or "abstract," often enables researchers to determine whether or not an article is indeed useful for their

purposes without having to locate and read it. This can be especially important when researchers are working in a library with a small periodical collection and must depend on interlibrary loans to acquire a significant number of articles.

There is a general abstract volume which covers broad topics in the field of sociology. Almost all of these abstracts are derived from sociological journals. This abstract is:

Sociological Abstracts. New York: Sociological Abstracts, 1952-.

    This source indexes and summarizes over 6,000 books and journal articles each year. Within broad subject areas, such as group interaction, social differentiation, and feminist studies, abstracts are arranged alphabetically by author. The last issue of each year contains cumulative author and subject indexes. The abstract is currently issued five times a year.

A specialized abstract is useful to sociologists because it covers a particular topic in greater detail and because it cites research which is published outside the field of sociology. An example of such an abstract volume is:

Criminal Justice Abstracts. Hackensack, N. J.: National Council on Crime and Delinquency, 1968-.

    This quarterly (formerly entitled Crime and Delinquency Literature through 1976) abstracts books and journals in the area of crime and delinquency. Abstracts are arranged under broad subject areas such as correction and law enforcement. There is a detailed subject index. Each issue also contains a review of current developments in one area, e.g., aid to victims, employee theft, delinquency prevention, etc.

Chapter 5

ABSTRACTS AND INDEXES

Assignment

1. Describe a situation in which an index or an abstract
    would be useful to a sociology student.

2. What is the basic difference between indexes and abstracts?

3. In your seminar on social issues, the instructor has
    developed a list of topics to be covered in class. To
    update the text, he has asked each student to compile a
    list of recent articles on one of the topics which will
    be distributed to the other students in the class. Your
    assigned topic is _____

    _____. You began your search with
    the most recent issue of Social Sciences Index, and have
    progressed to _____.

    a. What is the complete citation (author, title, journal,
        volume, date, and pages) for the first article listed
        on your topic? (Do not abbreviate the title of the
        journal.)

    b. On which page did you find this information?

4. In your world population course, you are comparing the
    recent internal migration patterns among several different
    countries. Each student is assigned a different country
    and asked to locate information dealing with this topic for

class comparison. Your country is _____.
One of the sources you consult is Population Index. Beginning with the most recent issues, you have progressed to the
_____ edition.

a. Using the cumulated geographic index, identify the title
   of the first publication in the English language which
   deals with this topic.

b. On what page did you find this item listed?

5. Your independent study project is on the topic _____
   _____.
   You want summaries of scholarly work done on the topic, so
   you consult Sociological Abstracts for _____.

a. Find the summary or abstract of the first article which
   studies this topic, and list the title and author.

b. On what page did you find this abstract?

6. One of the requirements for your course on crime and
   delinquency is a research paper. Thus far in researching
   your topic, _____,
   the sources you have found are somewhat outdated. To
   update these you consult Criminal Justice Abstracts. You
   begin with the most recent issues and have progressed to
   _____.

a. Locate the first item on this topic and list the title.

b. On what page did you find the summary of this item?

7. You are doing some preliminary reading for an independent study project. You find an article by _____ _____ which appeared in _____ _____.
Since this article deals with issues specifically on your topic, you want to see if any additional research has been completed which uses this article as a basis. You began with the most recent issue of Social Sciences Citation Index and have progressed to _____.
What is the author and title of the first article which refers to the article you have already located? (You must use two different sections of this index to answer this question.)

Chapter 6

BIBLIOGRAPHIES

Objective 1: After reading this chapter, the student will
describe a situation in which bibliographies
are useful for sociological study or research.

Objective 2: Given a subject, the student will use the
Bibliographic Index to identify an appropriate
bibliography appended to a book or article.

Objective 3: Given a subject, the student will use International
Bibliography of Sociology to identify an appropriate bibliography.

Objective 4: Given a subject, the student will use the Library
of Congress Subject Catalog to identify a book
on that subject.

To use study and independent research time effectively,

students should consult sources which identify existing print

materials relevant to their topics. In this regard, bibliog-

raphies constitute a particularly important category of finding

aids. An individual bibliography might list any or all of

the following: books, periodicals, periodical articles,

published documents, unpublished documents, or unpublished

manuscripts. The focus of the discussion in this chapter is

on bibliographies as finding aids, primarily for books other

than reference books and, secondarily, for articles. It should

be emphasized that whenever students use a bibliography that

does not list journal articles as well as book titles, they

must also consult a periodical index or abstract (see Chapter

Five) in order to compile a thorough reading list on the topic.

Some bibliographies provide only citations for the books

and articles they list; others provide annotations as well.

Standard bibliographic citation form for journal articles
includes author, title, journal name, volume and number, and
date of publication. In most cases, the information is
sufficiently complete to enable the researcher to locate the
item. Annotated bibliographies provide an additional service,
affording students a basis for deciding whether an individual
title might be useful. An annotation consists of a brief
summary of the article or book's content along with a comment
on its quality.

Whether annotated or not, bibliographies can appear in
two different formats: some are relatively short and are
appended to articles or books; others are book-length. The
purpose of the appended bibliography is to identify titles
that are either cited in the article or book or are relevant
to the topic being discussed. Students can profitably use a
bibliography appended to a reliable book or article as a guide
to their readings on the topic. To identify appended bibliographies on a particular topic, students may consult:

Bibliographic Index. New York: H. W. Wilson Co., 1937-.

Published in April and August and in a cumulated
annual volume in December, this work lists, by subject,
bibliographies with 50 or more entries which are published
separately or as parts of books or periodicals in English
and west European languages. Citations specify whether or
not the bibliographies are annotated. Each volume begins
with a prefatory note which briefly explains the forms
used in the entries.

The Bibliographic Index also identifies book-length bibliographies. The scope of these bibliographies is ordinarily

wider than that of appended bibliographies. Some book-length
bibliographies are published only once and are retrospective
in nature. An example of this type is <u>International Bibliography of Research in Marriage and the Family</u> (see Appendix).
Others are published periodically, sometimes annually, and
are called current bibliographies. The distinctive feature
of a current bibliography is that it is always being brought
up-to-date. Each new edition lists titles that have appeared
since the previous edition. However, most current bibliographies have a one to two year lag between the publication of a
book and its citation.

Among the most useful current bibliographies are those
which attempt coverage of a particular academic discipline,
such as sociology, or a group of related disciplines, such as
social sciences. In most cases, the coverage includes articles
as well as books, and the scope is international. Sociology
students should be familiar with:

<u>International Bibliography of Sociology</u>. London:
Tavistock, 1951-.

One of a set entitled <u>International Bibliography of
the Social Sciences</u>, this volume attempts to provide
comprehensive coverage of scholarly publications in the
field, regardless of country of origin, language, or
type. Three to five thousand citations are arranged in
a detailed classification scheme, with author and subject
indexes providing complete access. Citations are not
annotated. All information is given in French and English.
Although the volume is published each year, there is a
one to two year time lag.

If students are unable to identify or gain access to
bibliographies on their topics which are sufficiently compre-

hensive and up-to-date, they can turn to the bibliography of a national library to meet their needs. National libraries, such as the British Library or the Library of Congress, house copies of most of the important books on all subjects which are available in that country. Therefore, the subject catalogue of the Library of Congress, available in most college and university libraries, can be used as a reasonably comprehensive current bibliography on most topics.

> U. S. Library of Congress. <u>Subject Catalog: A Cumulative List of Works Represented by Library of Congress Printed Cards</u>. Washington, D. C.: 1950-.
>
> Published in quarterly, yearly, and five-year cumulative editions since 1950, the <u>Subject Catalog</u> lists books cataloged by the Library of Congress and other major libraries in the United States. Each edition offers the single most comprehensive bibliography of works on every subject (excluding works of fiction), and from all parts of the world, which have become available during the period it covers. Subject headings are cross-referenced.

Since the scope of the <u>Subject Catalog</u> is so broad, students should consult this source only when bibliographies related to their topic are not available, or after consulting the more topically-related bibliographies.

Chapter 6

BIBLIOGRAPHIES

Assignment

1. Describe a situation in which bibliographies are useful for sociological research.

2. In your seminar on the sociology of deviance, you are compiling a reading list for a term paper on _____ _____. You consult the Bibliographic Index to locate bibliographies appended to books or articles which address the topic. You begin with the most recent editions of that source and have progressed to the _____ edition.

   a. Who is the author and what is the title of the first book which has an appended bibliography relevant to your topic?

   b. On what page did you find this information?

3. You are required to write a term paper in your political sociology course. Since international relations and politics is an area that interests you, you choose the topic _____ for your paper. You begin with the most recent edition of the International Bibliography of Sociology, and have progressed to _____.

   a. Who is the author and what is the title of the first English language book or article that covers your topic?

b. On what page did you find this information?

4. For your senior thesis, you have decided to write a paper on some aspect of _____. For your working bibliography, you want to find all the books which are available. You have consulted more specialized sources and are now using the Subject Catalog. You began your search with the most recent edition and have reached the _____ edition.

a. What is the complete citation for the first English language title? (A complete citation includes author, title, place of publication, publisher, date of publication.)

b. In what volume and on what page did you find this information?

Chapter 7

GENERAL PERIODICALS AND NEWSPAPERS

Objective 1: After reading this chapter, the student will
              describe a situation in which a sociologist
              would use a general periodical or newspaper for
              research.
Objective 2: Given a topic and a time period, the student
              will use an index to identify the date, page,
              column, and summary information for a relevant
              article in the New York Times.
Objective 3: Given a specific topic, the student will locate
              articles from different newspapers which cover
              the topic, using NewsBank.
Objective 4: Given the citation for an article in Society,
              the student will locate specified information.

Students generally turn to book-length treatments of a

topic when they are doing independent reading or engaging in

research. The purpose of this chapter and the one following

is to suggest the considerable utility of periodicals and news-

papers.

The term "periodical" rather than "magazine" is used in

libraries because it more accurately identifies what is being

described: a publication which appears in print at regular

intervals during the year. There are two major types of

periodicals that are useful to sociologists: general periodicals

and scholarly periodicals or journals. The utility of the

latter will be discussed in the next chapter.

A general periodical is a publication containing articles

on a range of topics brought together to attract a large number

of general readers with varied interests. News magazines,

hobby or recreational magazines, and a host of publications
such as the Saturday Review and the New Yorker are all classified as general periodicals. A student can find information
on specific topics covered in general periodicals by consulting
the Readers' Guide to Periodical Literature.

General periodicals can not only broaden a student's knowledge and outlook, but can also serve a legitimate research
function for sociologists. Many general periodicals include
regular features on important social problems (such as poverty,
unemployment, or busing) and public opinion (attitudes toward
marijuana smoking, abortion, etc.). Among the major general
periodicals which are nonsociological but which emphasize social
and political affairs are the New York Times Magazine, the
Atlantic Monthly, and Harper's.

While general periodicals report current events and issues
of interest to the sociologist in jargon-free language, most
do not analyze them from a sociological perspective. However,
one general periodical which performs this function is:

> Society. (Formerly: Transaction: Social Science and
> Modern Society.) New Brunswick, N. J.: Rutgers-The
> State University, 1967-.
>
>   Written for the layperson by well-known sociologists
>   and other social scientists, this periodical covers a wide
>   variety of topics in the areas of government, housing,
>   welfare, law, race relations, and education. Issued
>   monthly.

Newspapers are regularly issued publications (daily,
weekly, semi-weekly) which report events and discuss topics of
current interest. The types of information which sociologists

may find useful are: news items, factual reporting of events; editorials, representing the editor's or the editorial board's thinking on current issues; feature articles, presenting an extensive investigation of a topic; and columns, expressing comments or reports on current events or issues by well-known journalists. For example, a student can find factual information on topics such as crime or intergroup conflict. Also, a student can identify attitudes of people toward important social issues.

A few newspapers are distinguished for the extensive coverage they give to national affairs, most notably the Washington Post and the New York Times. A student can find articles which cover specific topics in the New York Times by consulting its index:

New York Times Index. New York: New York Times, 1913-.

Provides subject access to New York Times news stories, editorials, and other features. Published every two weeks, it is cumulated annually. Each entry begins with a subject, followed by references to other sections in the index (if there are any). Then the article is summarized. For the sake of brevity, the citation identifies each month by one or two letters, followed by the date, a roman number for a section and an arabic page number, and sometimes a column number, prefaced by a colon. The year is always identified on the cover and title page and is essential information to record when copying citations. One important item to note in using this index is that the cross references which directly follow the subject in each entry must be checked in the index to obtain a complete citation. The user cannot identify the exact location of the articles noted in this section without doing so.

A sociology student may want coverage of an important topic from a number of different perspectives. In this

situation, a local newspaper or the New York Times would not
suit the student's needs. For example, the student may want
to compare the coverage of busing presented in a Southern
newspaper to that presented in a Northern newspaper. When
confronted with that type of situation the student should
consult:

> NewsBank: Urban Affairs Library. Greenwich, Conn.:
> 1975-.
>
> This publication not only indexes articles on
> subjects from over 150 daily and weekly urban newspapers,
> but also includes the articles themselves on microfiche.
> The index is divided into 13 subject sections--Business
> and Economic Development, Consumer Affairs, Government
> Structure, Social Relations, Welfare and Poverty, Housing
> and Urban Renewal, Law and Order, Education, Political
> Development, Health, Transportation, Environment, and
> Employment--each contained in separate binders. The
> microfiche copies of the articles are located in the
> back of each binder. Note that there is a separate
> binder containing an Introduction, Guide to the Index,
> and an overall Name Index. The Guide to the Index
> section is designed as an aid to determine in which of
> the 13 major subject categories a particular topic is
> covered. A cumulative subject index for each topical
> area is provided annually.

Chapter 7

GENERAL PERIODICALS AND NEWSPAPERS

Assignment

1. Describe a situation in which it would be appropriate to use a general periodical or newspaper for research.

2. In your social psychology course, the instructor has stressed that our perception of social issues and phenomena is heavily influenced by our values, and our values are influenced by the geographical area in which we live. To test this assertion, he asks each student to find a newspaper article from two different states dealing with the same topic.

    a. Using NewsBank for the year 1975, what are the microfiche numbers for the first articles on _____ _____ for _____ _____ and _____?

    b. What is the title of the article for the first state listed above? (You must go to the microfiche to find this.)

3. In your social problems course, the instructor has asked each person to pick a specific social issue, then to summarize the major events for a given year. One of the works you use to compile a list of sources of information is the New York Times Index. On a separate card, you take down the summary and citation for any news stories you think you may want to consult. You have chosen the topic _____ _____ for the year _____.

a. What is the summary of the first story listed under your topic?

b. What is the complete citation for that story (month, day, page, column)?

4. During a lecture in your contemporary American society course, the instructor recommends an article entitled _____ in the _____ issue of Society which presents a highly readable discussion of the topic.

a. Who is the author of the article?

b. What is the academic affiliation of the major author?

Chapter 8

SCHOLARLY JOURNALS

Objective 1: After reading this chapter, the student will describe the principal uses of sociology journals.

Objective 2: Given a specific issue of a journal, the student will answer questions about its content and format.

Objective 3: Using Magazines for Libraries, the student will identify the first index or abstract which covers that journal.

The purpose of this chapter is to describe the use of a special type of periodical--the scholarly journal. Through the articles and book reviews they contain, scholarly journals serve important functions, making them an especially valuable source of information for students, particularly as they undertake independent study or research.

The articles in scholarly journals, written by specialists and critically evaluated by other scholars prior to being accepted for publication, often represent the most recent additions to an academic discipline's shared store of knowledge or to its debate on a particular topic. An article may deal with a topic that has not yet been treated and may never be treated in a book-length publication; on the other hand it may contain new information about, or a new interpretation of, a subject already covered in book-length publications. In either case, students interested in compiling a well-rounded and up-to-date reading list on a topic often can insure those qualities only if they seek out articles on the topic in scholarly journals. Students should remember, however, that the articles in these journals are written for a specialized audience; therefore they may employ some concepts or methodological procedures which are unfamiliar.

Most scholarly journals contain a book review section where scholars in the field present critiques of the books recently published by their colleagues. Since the reviewer is generally a person who has studied the topic, these reviews usually give an accurate assessment of the book's quality from a sociological standpoint. Also, reviews, by summarizing the content of the books, enable the student to decide about their utility for research or independent study. When faced with a choice of several books, the student can save time by utilizing book reviews to select the most useful, authoritative sources.

Sociologists publish a large number of journals, some rather general in scope, and some devoted to a particular subfield within the discipline, such as family studies. The following are journals with which the sociology student should be familiar:

American Journal of Sociology. Chicago: University of Chicago Press, 1895-.

This bi-monthly journal reports research and field work on a variety of topics in sociology. The articles range from 12 to 50 pages, though the average length is approximately 27 pages. Short papers which summarize recent empirical research are included in a "Research Notes" section. Each issue also contains a comprehensive book review section with evaluative signed reviews.

American Sociological Review. Washington, D. C.: American Sociological Association, 1936-.

    The official journal of the American Sociological Association, this bi-monthly publication contains articles which cover all areas of sociology. The average length of articles is 12 pages. The journal also reports the activities of the Association and contains a section for comments and discussions of previous articles.

Social Forces. Chapel Hill, N. C.: University of North Carolina Press, 1922-.

    This quarterly, which contains articles averaging 20 pages in length, includes all aspects of sociology. The journal is international in scope, but articles about the United States predominate. Each issue contains a number of signed book reviews. Special issues, in which all the articles focus upon a specific topic, appear at least once a year.

Though these are major sociology journals, they represent a small fraction of the scholarly periodicals published by sociologists. A student can find a brief description of a number of other scholarly journals within sociology, as well as within other academic disciplines, by consulting:

Katz, William. Magazines for Libraries. 3rd ed. New York: Bowker, 1978.

    This work contains publication information and descriptive and evaluative annotations for over 6,500 periodicals and newspapers. Titles are organized into approximately 100 subject areas, such as: Aeronautics Space Science, Africa, Business Education, General Magazines, Government Magazines, History, Opinion Magazines, and Newspapers. Because of this topical organization, the volume's index is particularly useful for locating individual titles.

Chapter 8

SCHOLARLY JOURNALS

Assignment

1. Describe a situation in which it would be appropriate
    to use a sociological journal.

    In your sociology resources and methods course, your
    instructor wants each student to become familiar with
    the format of some of the important sociology journals.
    As an exercise, she gives each student a list of spe-
    cific issues of several journals and a set of questions
    about each issue. You have been assigned the following:

2. American Journal of Sociology, _____.

    a. Who is the author of the article entitled _____
        _____?

    b. Where does the author teach?

    c. Where was this material originally presented?

3. American Sociological Review, _____.

    a. What is the title of the article by _____
        _____?

b. What is the complete citation for the first publication listed in the bibliography of the article?

4. <u>Social Forces</u>, _____.

a. Who wrote the book review of _____
_____?

b. With what institution is the reviewer affiliated?

c. Identify the page numbers where the review appears.

5. Your instructor has recommended an article related to your
term paper topic that appeared in the journal _____
_____. He is unable to remember
the exact title or the author of the article and your
library does not own this journal. You need to know where
the journal is indexed so that you can find a complete
citation for this article. Using <u>Magazines for Libraries</u>,
find the entry for this journal.

a. In what source can you find articles from this journal
indexed or abstracted? (List the first, if there is
more than one, and given the full title, <u>not</u> the
abbreviation.)

b. On what page did you find this information?

Chapter 9

EVALUATING BOOK-LENGTH STUDIES

Objective 1: After reading this chapter, the student will explain the necessity for evaluating research sources and will describe one method for doing so.

Objective 2: Given the author, title, and publication date for a book, the student, using the Social Sciences Index, will identify a periodical containing a review of the book.

Objective 3: Given the author, title, and publication date for a book, the student will locate a review in Contemporary Sociology.

Book-length studies will in most cases constitute the greater part of a student's reading list on an individual research or independent study topic. Finding aids which students may use to identify book titles appropriate to a particular topic were discussed in Chapter Six. Much depends upon the care with which students select from among the titles they do identify; if the sources of information used in research and study are unreliable, the results will necessarily be unsatisfactory. There are two principal ways for a student to go about the task of evaluating a book-length study of a particular topic: by relying upon book reviews and by examining the bibliographic quality of the book itself.

Book Review Sources

Since 1975, reviews appearing in most of the major sociology journals have been indexed in the book review section of the Social Sciences Index (see Chapter Five). The reviews are indexed by the name of the author of the book; the journal, volume and date, and the page of the review are provided.

There is generally a considerable time lag, sometimes more than a year, between the publication of a book and the appearance of a review in a scholarly journal. The need for more current reviews has given rise to a new type of journal, which consists entirely of scholarly book reviews. The journal which fulfills this need for sociologists is:

> Contemporary Sociology: A Journal of Reviews. Washington, D. C.: American Sociological Association, 1971-.
>
> This journal reviews books published in every area of sociology plus many in related fields, such as education. Each issue also contains feature essays which review several books on related topics or the works of one major author. The reviews are arranged by broad subject areas, and each issue also contains a list of new publications.

Bibliographic Character of the Work

By examining certain features of a book closely, a student can often accurately assess the quality of the information presented. The preface and introduction usually tell something about who the author is, why the work was written, and what methodology and research went into the preparation of the work. If the author is an acknowledged authority in the field, this is often mentioned in the work itself.

The footnotes and the quality of the bibliography (or in some cases, the lack of one) can also be relied upon as clues about the reliability of the work. If few or no original documents have been used, or if major works in the field have not been either cited or evaluated, the student has reason to question the quality of the work.

Finally, the reputation of the publisher or organization which sponsors a particular book can provide the student a clue to the reliability of the information it contains. Some publishers have more rigid standards of scholarship than others. For example, the requirements of university presses are generally very high, and the major university presses, such as Cambridge, Chicago, Michigan, and Harvard, can be counted on as disciminating publishers of studies in sociology.

Chapter 9

EVALUATING BOOK-LENGTH STUDIES

Assignment

1. Explain why a sociology major would need to evaluate
    research sources and describe one method for doing so.

2. You are writing a paper and discover that you are relying
    heavily upon _____
    _____ by _____
    for portions of your analysis. You decide that you would
    like to know how other sociologists have evaluated the
    book. To locate a review, you turn to the book review
    section of the Social Sciences Index (annotated in Chapter
    Five). Using _____,
    give the complete citation (journal, volume, pages, date,
    and reviewer) of the first book review listed. (Do not
    abbreviate the name of the journal.)

3. For your independent study course, you are preparing a
    review of the recent literature on an assigned topic.
    Since you have identified a number of books on this topic
    and want to select the best to actually read, you decide
    to locate scholarly reviews of each book. One of your
    books is _____
    _____ by _____.
    You have located a review in Contemporary Sociology, ____
    _____.

    a. Who is the author of the review?

    b. What is the institutional affiliation of the reviewer?

    c. On what page(s) does the review appear?

Chapter 10

UNITED STATES GOVERNMENT PUBLICATIONS

Objective 1: After reading this chapter, the student will describe a situation in which government publications would be useful for sociological research.

Objective 2: Given a topic, the student will use the CIS/Index to Publications of the United States Congress to locate a congressional hearing and give specific information about it.

Objective 3: The student will identify a United States government publication on a specific topic using the Monthly Catalog and the Cumulative Subject Index to the Monthly Catalog.

This chapter and the following chapter on census publications introduce students to the variety and uses of United States government publications. These comprise all the printed public documents of the federal government. The materials include, for example: the offical records of the meetings of the United States Congress; the text of laws, of court decisions, and of public hearings and rulings of administrative and regulatory agencies; studies of economic and social issues commissioned by offical agencies; and the compilation of statistics on a number of social and demographic characteristics of the United States population. The discussion of the utility of this latter type of publication--the compilation of statistics and data--will be reserved for the following chapter.

Federal publications afford sociologists and sociology students material for research in many subfields in sociology. Students can find government publications, in one form or another, which cover such topics as the educational attainment of minorities, planned parenthood, sex discrimination, drug abuse, and a number of other social issues. When using United States government publications, students should, of course, exercise normal scholarly caution. The fact that a document is "official" is no automatic guarantee of the accuracy of the information or data it might contain. The accuracy depends on the methods of information and data collection the agency used, as well as the situation in which the agency operated. Therefore, the use of these publications, like the use of any other source material, requires good judgement. It also requires familiarity with the methods and means for identifying and gaining access to individual publications relevant to a particular topic.

Students can identify relevant late nineteenth and twentieth century federal government publications by consulting:

U. S. Superintendent of Documents. Monthly Catalog of United States Government Publications. Washington, D. C.: Government Printing Office, 1885-.

This is the most complete catalogue of federal documents available. The detailed indexes--subject, author/agency, and title--identify individual items by entry number. Entries identify personal author (if any), pagination, date, illustration notes, series title, serial number, and include reference to any other publication superceded by this item, and the Superintendent of Documents number. (United States documents are arranged by this number in many libraries, especially those that are depositories.)

Cumulative Subject Index to the Monthly Catalog of United States Government Publications, 1900-1971. Washington, D. C.: Carrollton Press, 1973.

This is a comprehensive subject index to more than one million publications listed in the Monthly Catalog

from 1900 through 1971. To discover what has been
published on a given subject, one first finds the topic
and then goes to the appropriate subheading. This will
be followed by one or more years in parentheses, each
followed by one or more entry numbers (e.g., (65) 14901).
Then researchers must turn to the Monthly Catalog for
the specified year (in this case, 1965) and locate the
entry number (in this case, 14901) in order to find
a complete citation for the publication.

Given the vast number of United States government publications, there are, not surprisingly, a great number of
sources which identify individual titles. Therefore, the
first task for researchers is to select reference sources
appropriate to their needs. The most useful list and
discussion of finding aids for United States publications in
the area of social science is U. S. Government Publications
Relating to the Social Sciences by Joseph K. Lu (see Appendix
for complete citation).

An awareness of the factors which influence the United
States government's policies toward various social issues
(e.g., busing, welfare, minority rights) is essential to the
sociologist. Political policy is formulated by political
officials and influenced by citizens or groups of citizens,
all of whom are concerned about a specific issue. For this
reason, the records of congressional hearings are valuable
sources of information to the sociology student. These
records provide important policy-related information: they
reveal the political stands that various citizens or groups
take on a specific issue; and they demonstrate, albeit indi-
rectly, the influence these persons have on the formulation

of public policy. Since the persons who testify at these
hearings have special knowledge of, or expertise in, a topic,
the students can learn the facts and viewpoints surrounding
an issue. The records of Congressional hearings can be
located by using:

CIS/Index to Publications of the United States Congress.
Washington, D. C.: James B. Adler, 1970-.

    The CIS/Index has become, within a few years, a
basic source for the working papers of Congress. It
provides information in the form of abstracts of
congressional documents, and microfiche copies of the
documents themselves. It covers the entire range of
congressional publications, which is to say approximately 400,000 pages a year of hearings, committee
prints, House and Senate reports, and other congressional
documents.

    The CIS/Index is issued in two sections--the indexes
and abstracts--and is cumulated quarterly and annually.
To locate specific materials or information on a
specific topic, first turn to the index section. Key
word titles are listed in the index with entry numbers
which can be used to locate the abstract and microfiche
copy of the publication.

    A similar publication issued by the same company,
the American Statistics Index (see next chapter for
complete citation) indexes statistics published by
government agencies on numerous topics in thousands of
publications each year.

Chapter 10

UNITED STATES GOVERNMENT PUBLICATIONS

Assignment

1. Describe a situation in which United States government publications would be useful for sociological research.

2. The instructor in your social problems course has asked each student to locate a current discussion of an important social issue and to summarize the content of the discussion. One source of such discussions are congressional hearings. Your instructor assigns you the topic _____ and asks you to find a hearing for _____.

    a. Using CIS/Index to Publications of the United States Congress, what is the index number of the first entry which addresses this topic?

    b. On what page can you find a summary or abstract of this hearing?

    c. What is the name of the first witness at the hearing and his/her official position? (You must use the abstract section of the index to answer this question.)

3. For your perspectives on poverty seminar you are doing a paper on _____.
You have already identified books and articles pertaining to the topic and are now checking to see if any relevant publications have been issued by the federal government. To check quickly the 1900-1971 period, you begin with the Cumulative Subject Index to the Monthly Catalog.

    a. What is the Monthly Catalog year and entry number for the first entry on your topic?

    b. What are the title, copyright date, and number of pages of that publication?

Chapter 11

UNITED STATES CENSUS PUBLICATIONS

Objective 1:   The student will describe a situation in which
               a United States Census Bureau publication
               would be useful in sociological research.
Objective 2:   Given a topic, the student will use <u>American</u>
               <u>Statistics Index</u> to locate a United States
               government statistical publication which covers
               it.
Objective 3:   Using the <u>Bureau of the Census Catalog</u>, the
               student will locate a publication which studies
               a specific population characteristic.

The compilation and analysis of data are two essential

research tasks for sociologists. Generally, sociologists

who do quantitative research are interested in generating

statistics on various social, demographic, or social psycho-

logical characteristics of specific population groups. United

States Census Bureau publications are important resources

because they allow sociologists and sociology students to

summarize the social and demographic characteristics of

different population groups in the United States by using

descriptive statistics.

Students frequently think of the Census Bureau as a

government agency whose sole task is the massive collection

of census data every ten years. There are actually 10 types

or categories of censuses, and the data are collected and

reported at different intervals. Besides collecting data

on national and state populations, the Census Bureau also

studies specific subpopulations that are of special interest to government agencies. These studies are generally part of a series published in Current Population Reports. Recent reports, for example, have focused upon the characteristics of blacks, persons of Spanish origin, and poverty-level families.

Census publications provide, at little cost to the researcher, a wealth of descriptive information on various components of the American population. It would be very costly and time-consuming for a researcher to compile data comparable to that of the Census Bureau. However, there are some drawbacks to census data of which students should be aware. Most data are compiled every five or ten years; as a result, a researcher either must find more current information or use the somewhat dated statistics published by the Census Bureau. Also, the design of the census survey may not include the types of questions or issues that are of interest to the sociologist or sociology student. For example, a student comparing the educational or employment status of blacks with that of persons of Spanish origin would not be able to do so by using the 1970 census data because the 1970 Census of Population did not allow persons of Spanish origin to identify their racial or ethnic background. A final disadvantage of census publications is that they use descriptive statistics to summarize the data. A researcher, then, can determine social and demographic differences in a population, but not the causes of these differences.

Because the Census Bureau analyzes and publishes so much

data, students can locate relevant census materials most
effectively by consulting guides and indexes to statistical
reports published by the government. A comprehensive volume
which indexes statistical studies by all government agencies
and that can be used to locate a variety of statistics on a
given topic is:

American Statistics Index. Washington, D. C.: Congressional Information Service, 1973-.

 This commercially produced abstract has become an
important source for identifying statistical publications published by the United States government. It
indexes and abstracts statistics on numerous topics
from the publications of many government agencies,
describes these publications, and makes the material
available on microfiche.

 This source is issued monthly in two sections--
indexes and abstracts--and is cumulated annually. The
index volume contains four separate indexes that list
the publications by subject and name; by geographic,
economic, and demographic categories; by title; and by
agency report numbers. The abstract volume gives
brief descriptions of the publications and their content.

The Census Bureau publishes an index to its own publications. If students want specific information on a topic or
characteristic that is routinely studied by the Census Bureau,
they should consult:

U. S. Bureau of the Census. Bureau of the Census Catalog.
Washington, D. C.: Government Printing Office, 1790-.

 An indispensible guide to materials issued by the
Bureau of the Census and publications from other agencies
which contain statistics, this catalog is published
quarterly, updated with monthly supplements, and has
annual cumulations. The basic volume is retrospective,
covering the years 1790-1945 in part I, and 1946-1972 in
part II. The arrangement differs in each part. The
material covered includes annotated lists of census

publications for the years covered, followed by subject
and geographical indexes.

The annual cumulation lists and annotates only
those publications issued during that year. It also is
divided into two parts. Part I is a classified list of
materials by broad subject areas and has a geographical
and subject index. In broad subject areas, part II
lists data files, special tabulations, and includes
some unpublished nonstatistical materials. No index is
included in this section.

A number of reports or volumes published by the Census

Bureau are useful to sociologists or sociology students doing

research. Several of these publications--the County and City

Data Book, the Statistical Abstracts of the United States,

and the Historical Statistics of the United States--have

been discussed in previous chapters. These publications

summarize many of the important findings of past censuses, as

well as recent ones. A student who wants a complete descrip-

tion of the social or demographic characteristics of the pop-

ulation for a specific time period should consult the population

census.

Besides the population census (see Appendix), the bureau

also conducts surveys of housing, business, and manufacturing.

A student who wants information about the structural or indus-

trial characteristics of the United States can use these

censuses to find current statistics. These censuses have the

advantages and disadvantages of the 1970 Census of Population

discussed earlier.

Chapter 11

UNITED STATES CENSUS PUBLICATIONS

Assignment

1. Describe a situation in which a sociologist would use a Census Bureau publication.

2. The instructor in your contemporary social problems course has assigned a term paper. You have chosen the topic _____.
    To support your assertions with relevant data you consult the American Statistics Index. You began with the most recent issue and are now using _____.

    a. What is the abstract number for the first publication listed under your topic?

    b. On what page(s) of the publication can you find a table with information on your topic? (List the pages of the first table is there is more than one.)

3. One of the assignments in your population course asks you to develop a list of sources which contain statistics about a specific population characteristic. You have been assigned the population characteristic _____ _____. Using the Bureau of the Census Catalog for _____, answer the following:

    a. On what page do you find a publication which studies this topic?

    b. What is the length of this publication?

Chapter 12

RESEARCH PAPER MECHANICS AND METHODOLOGY

Objective 1: After reading this chapter, the student will utilize the techniques and strategies presented to accomplish the prepatory work for a research paper, up to and including the compilation of a bibliography. Specifically, the student will:

(a) narrow a topic down;
(b) identify and use reference works such as encyclopedias for background information;
(c) develop a list of appropriate subject headings to use in indexes, abstracts, the subject catalogue, etc.;
(d) identify and use appropriate indexes, abstracts, bibliographies;
(e) utilize other resources to full advantage, for example by exploiting bibliographies and footnotes in books and articles and the information on a catalogue card;
(f) maintain a search record;
(g) prepare bibliography cards, using standard citation forms.

The topic of a research paper should be chosen carefully. The student should consider the following questions at the start, rather than after much time has been spent doing research; for if the answers to them are negative, research time already spent may prove to have been time wasted.

Can the topic be <u>investigated</u> well?

For most college or university research papers, this reduces to the question of whether there is sufficient research material relevant to the topic available locally--either housed in area libraries or easily obtainable through interlibrary loan.

Can the project be _done_ well?

There are objective and subjective factors to consider here. Among the former, perhaps the most important is the scope of the research topic. Students who take on topics that are too large will end with superficial research in available sources, and inevitably, superficial and incomplete treatments of their topic in their papers. As an example, suppose that a student wants to do a research paper on effects of parental socialization on the values of their children. Soon after the student begins the search process, it will be discovered that there are more research references than can be adequately covered in the allotted time. The topic chosen is too broad; it does not specify a focal time period or era, and it does not clearly indicate the number of factors or "variables" that will be studied in depth. The more voluminous the research in a particular subject area, such as family socialization patterns, the greater is the likelihood that a student will encounter this type of problem, and therefore the more the focal time period or the number of variables will have to be restricted. The student might feasibly narrow the topic and begin the search process on one of the following: socialization patterns in the 1960s; parental socialization during the Great Depression; socialization in the black family; socialization in single-parent families; or families in poverty.

In addition to selecting topics that will not conflict with time requirements, it is advisable for students to select topics about which they know something initially; which are capable of holding their interest; and which will require them to evaluate, form judgements, and come to definite conclusions. These considerations--about interests and requirements--may be important determinants of the amount of work students are willing to do, and the amount of satisfaction with which they will do it.

After selecting a topic, the time devoted to collecting information can be spent in the most efficient way possible if some basic library research techniques are utilized. Specifically, this chapter will focus on research mechanics (for example, copying complete citations on bibliography cards) and research methodology (for example, selecting appropriate reference tools).

MECHANICS

Complete Citations

Often research time is wasted back-tracking because certain mechanical tasks were not properly done initially. It is useful, for example, to copy, in correct form on separate cards, complete citations for every book, article, etc., for which a reference is found and which is, or might be, consulted. Among other things, this procedure will: (1) afford a complete, current record of sources which have been or will be used; (2) eliminate retracing steps later to find necessary bibliographic information on sources which have been used; (3) afford a record of sources which were not available during the initial search; (4) allow requests

for interlibrary loan to be filled without having to return
to the source for complete bibliographic information.
Finally, at the end, no source will have to be rechecked
for precise title, author, publication data, and other
information necessary to prepare an accurate bibliography for
the completed paper.

When citing books, articles, pamphlets, government publications, etc., sociology students should use the forms
suggested by the American Sociological Association. Examples
of the basic forms are:

Books

Johnstone, Ronald
   1975 Religion and Society in Interaction: The
         Sociology of Religion. Englewood Cliffs:
         Prentice Hall.

Articles

Gecas, Viktor and F. Ivan Nye
   1974 "Sex and class differences in parent-child inter-
         action: a test of Kohn's hypothesis." Journal
         of Marriage and the Family 36:742-49.

Government Publications

U. S. Department of Labor
   1975 "Marital and family characteristics of the labor
         force, March 1974." Special Labor Force Report
         173. Washington, D. C.: U. S. Government
         Printing Office.

Developing a Subject Heading List

During the initial stages of research, students should
develop a list of the subject headings they will use when
consulting the card catalogue, bibliographies, indexes, and

abstracts. An inclusive list of possible headings is advantageous because not all of these reference sources use the same subject headings for indexing. Thus, the more topical categories students have listed, the more likely they are to locate useful material in all of the reference sources they consult. For example, a student writing on family interaction patterns may find useful titles listed under:

Roles, marital

Family structure

Sex-role socialization

The Library of Congress Subject Headings (see Appendix for complete citation) is a useful source for quickly identifying a number of subject heading alternatives. This two-volume work contains a list of the headings which are used in the subject catalogues of most libraries. When beginning a research project, students should note the subject headings listed in this source and then, as the research proceeds, add new headings which seem appropriate.

Use of the Library Catalogue

The most frequent error made by students involved in a research project is to begin their investigation by turning to the subject section of their library's catalogue. Often this error is made because students do not understand the purposes and limitations of a library catalogue.

A library catalogue, simply put, is primarily an author,

title, and subject list of the book holdings of that library.
Because the budgets in individual libraries are limited and
the subject emphases of institutions differ, no library owns
a comprehensive collection (or even a collection of all the
best publications) on every topic. In addition, the subject
headings used by most libraries are general in nature and
limited in number for any given book (this is one reason for
the discussion of the subject heading list in the previous
section). Therefore, it is important for students involved
in research to recognize that the library's catalogue is
not generally the best place to begin a research project
and should be consulted only for specific purposes. These
include: (1) to determine whether the library owns a bibliography on the subject; (2) to determine whether or not the
library owns useful books identified through the use of bibliographies or other specialized reference works; or (3) to
determine whether the library owns titles on a topic published
more recently than the reference publications (guides, bibliographies, indexes) being consulted.

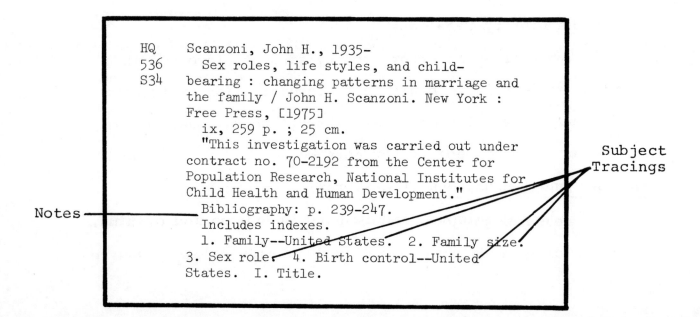

In addition to the call number, cards in the library's card catalogue provide other useful information. If a book has a bibliography or bibliographical footnotes, a brief note in the center of the card indicates that it does, and sometimes indicates the pages of the book on which the bibliography will be found. For example, the title on the card illustrated on the previous page has bibliographical notes from page 239-247. This information should be included on the bibliography card the student prepares for the book. Books with bibliographies should be examined first; the bibliographies may lead directly to useful sources and save the student a great deal of research time using more general reference sources.

The subject tracings on catalogue cards identify all the subject headings under which the book is listed in the subject section of the card catalogue. For the book in the example, cards are filed under Family--United States, Family size, Sex role, and Birth control--United States. The student who finds that the Scanzoni book is useful for a particular research project may find additional useful titles by checking the library's subject catalogue under these headings. (Subject heading tracings as they are identified should be added to the "Subject Heading List" suggested above.)

Keeping a Search Record

In research projects carried out over a period of time, students often redo some search work or miss valuable sources.

To save time and insure a thorough search, a research record should be kept. This can be done conveniently on three by five cards--one for each step in this research. An individual card should indicate one source (index, abstract, bibliography, etc.) and the subject headings and dates covered during the research. As an example:

<u>Sociological Abstracts</u>

Volumes Searched: v. 37 (1972) to v. 42
                   no. 4 (1977)

Topic: Parents, Children, and Socialization
        Patterns in the 1970s

Headings Used: Child -ren -hood
                Family -ies
                Marriage and Family
                Parent -s -al
                Socialization

In addition, students should maintain a general card that lists together, in abbreviated form, all sources used. These steps will eliminate the possibility of needless duplication of effort and can help insure a thorough coverage of available materials.

RESEARCH METHODOLOGY

Adequate initial planning is one of the more important requirements of efficient library research. The better the

methods, the greater the amount of information the student
is likely to locate in the time spent in the library. On
the following pages are flow charts which describe generalized
research strategies for locating books and periodicals for
a research paper. Not all papers will require using every
step, and not all library research is best accomplished by
using these strategies. These strategies can serve, however,
as suggestive examples for student researchers.

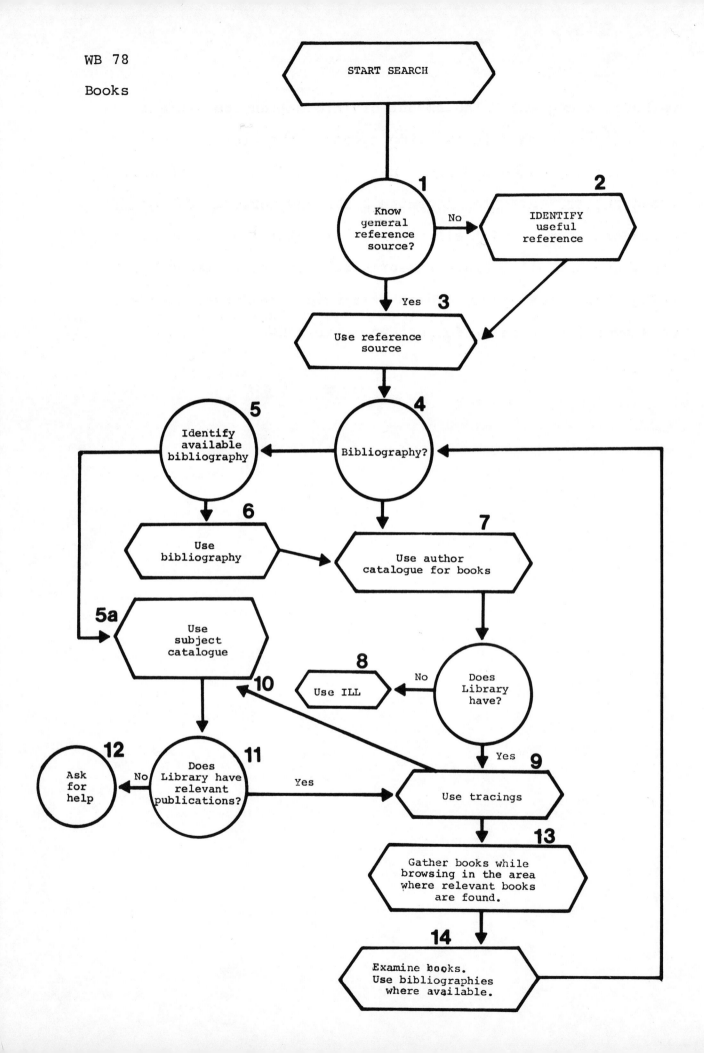

BOOKS FLOW CHART DIRECTIONS

1. When beginning research, identify a general source which supplies background information. Subject encyclopedias (Chapter Four), handbooks (Chapter Two), and textbooks are examples of publications useful at the start of a project.

2. If you do not know a general source, attempt to identify one by consulting a guide (see Chapter One). Also, your instructor or a librarian may be able to help you identify a general source.

3. With the aid of the general source, attempt to define your topic as precisely as possible, and

4. Prepare bibliography cards on relevant books and articles in the bibliography, if there is one in the general source.

5. If there is no bibliography in the general source, locate one by using a guide (see Chapter One), or one of the sources discussed in Chapter Six which identifies bibliographies, or consult with your instructor or a librarian, or

5a. Consult your library's subject catalogue. If your library owns a specialized bibliography on your topic, it will be listed under the subject with a subdivision for bibliography, e.g., Local Transit - Bibliography.

6. Having located a bibliography (for a discussion see Chapter Six), select materials which seem appropriate and make bibliography cards.

7. Check the author or title catalogue to determine whether your library owns the materials you identified through your previous efforts (for periodical articles listed, see step seven in the next flow chart).

8. If the library does not own some of the materials you need, request the materials through interlibrary loan (ask a librarian about procedures).

9. Use the card catalogue to determine which of the books you selected have bibliographies. Also, check the subject tracings and add new subject headings to your master list.

10-11. Using your master list of subject headings, consult your library's subject catalogue to determine whether the library has books relevant to your topic published since the bibliography you used; and for relevant books, copy complete citations, list pertinent notes, and look for any new subject tracings that would be useful.

12. If at this point you feel your bibliography is inadequate, see a librarian or your instructor to evaluate your research to this point.

13. Once you have identified relevant items owned by the library, go to the shelves, and, while gathering your books, examine others for which you have no citations but whose titles indicate they might deal with your topic.

14. As you begin using the books you have selected, check the bibliographies. If you do not have citations for some of the items you find, you may want to make additional bibliography cards and attempt to locate these materials later.

START SEARCH

1 Have cards listing articles?

No

2 Know appropriate Abstract or Index?

No

3 Select appropriate Abstract or Index

4 Use Abstract or Index

5 Are articles listed?

No

6 Ask for help

Yes

7 Use Library's List of Journals

8 Does Library own?

No

9 Use Interlibrary Loan

Yes

10 Read material, select relevant key words, bibliographic citations

Chapter 12

RESEARCH PAPER MECHANICS AND METHODOLOGY

Assignment

Select a topic and prepare a bibliography as if you were
going to write a twenty page research paper. The bibliography
should be on three by five cards using the style suggested
in this chapter. Along with the bibliography, turn in a
three to five page typed "journal" or "log" of your research
work. Write down each step that you take as you take it and
explain why you decided to take that step. For example, when
you consult a reference work, record its title, your reason
for consulting it and what, if any, use it was to you. Also,
turn in your research record cards and subject headings list.

Each bibliography should include: basic sources for
the topic; the major publications dealing with the topic; and
publications dealing with the most recent research. Each
topic must be approved in advance.

APPENDIX

Chapter 1 - Guides to the Literature

American Reference Books Annual. Edited by Bohdan S. Wynar. Littleton, Colo.: Libraries Unlimited, 1970-.

Freides, Thelma. Literature and Bibliography of the Social Sciences. Los Angeles: Molville, 1973.

Hoselitz, Bert F., ed. A Readers' Guide to the Social Sciences. rev. ed. New York: Free Pr., 1970.

McInnis, Raymond G. and James W. Scott. Social Science Research Handbook. New York: Barnes and Noble, 1974.

Chapter 2 - Handbooks

U. S. Bureau of the Census. Congressional District Data Book. Washington, D. C.: Government Printing Office, 1961/62-.

Christensen, Harold T., ed. Handbook of Marriage and the Family. Chicago: Rand McNally, 1964.

Faris, Robert E. L. Handbook of Modern Sociology. Chicago: Rand McNally, 1964.

March, James G., ed. Handbook of Organizations. Chicago: Rand McNally, 1965.

Hare, A. Paul. Handbook of Small Group Research. 2d ed. New York: Free Pr., 1976.

Goslen, David A. Handbook of Socialization Theory and Research. Chicago: Rand McNally, 1969.

Ogburn, William F. and Mayer F. Nimkoff. Handbook of Sociology. 5th ed. rev. London: Routledge, 1964.

Smigel, Erwin O., ed. Handbook on the Study of Social Problems. Chicago: Rand McNally, 1971.

Chapter 3 - Yearbooks

Municipal Year Book. Washington, D. C.: International
    City Management Association, 1934-.

Statistical Abstract of the United States. Washington, D. C.:
    Government Printing Office, 1878-.

Chapter 4 - Subject Dictionaries and Encyclopedias

Fairchild, Henry Pratt. Dictionary of Sociology and Related
    Sciences. Totawa, N. J.: Littlefield, Adams, 1970.

Gould, Julius and William L. Kolb, eds. A Dictionary of the
    Social Sciences. New York: Free Pr., 1964.

Encyclopaedia of the Social Sciences. New York: Macmillan,
    1930-1935. 15 vol.

Abrams, Charles. The Language of Cities: A Glossary of
    Terms. New York: Viking, 1971.

Theodorson, George A. and Achilles G. Theodorson. A Modern
    Dictionary of Sociology. New York: Crowell, 1969.

Chapter 5 - Abstracts and Indexes

Abstracts for Social Workers. Albany: National Association
    of Social Workers, 1965-.

C. R. I. S.: The Combined Retrospective Index Set to Journals
    in Sociology, 1895-1974. Washington, D. C.: Carrollton
    Pr., 1978. 6 vols.

Child Development Abstracts and Bibliography. Chicago:
    Society for Research in Child Development, 1927-.

Current Index to Journals in Education. Washington, D. C.:
    Government Printing Office, 1969-.

Education Index. New York: Wilson, 1929-.

Psychological Abstracts. Washington, D. C.: American Psycho-
    logical Association, 1927-.

Readers' Guide to Periodical Literature. New York: Wilson,
    1905-.

Resources in Education. Washington, D. C.: Government Printing
Office, 1966-.

Sage Urban Studies Abstracts. Beverly Hills: Sage, 1973-.

Women Studies Abstracts. New York: Rush, 1972-.

Chapter 6 - Bibliographies

Current Contents: Behavioral, Social and Management Sciences.
Philadelphia: Institute for Scientific Information, 1969-.

International Bibliography of Research in Marriage and the
Family, 1900-1964. Edited by Joan Aldous and Reuben
Hill. Minneapolis: University of Minnesota Pr., 1967.
Volume 2: 1965-1972. Compiled by Joan Aldous and
Nancy Dahl. Minneapolis: University of Minnesota Pr.,
1974.

Inventory of Marriage and Family Literature. St. Paul, Minn.:
Family Social Science, University of Minnesota, 1973/74-.

Women's Work and Women's Studies/1973-74: A Bibliography.
New York: Barnard College Women's Center, 1975.

Chapter 8 - Scholarly Journals

International Journal of Comparative Sociology. Leiden,
The Netherlands: E. J. Bell, 1960-.

Journal of Marriage and the Family. Minneapolis: National
Council on Family Relations, 1938-.

Journal of Social Issues. Ann Arbor, Mich.: Society for the
Psychological Study of Social Issues, 1945-.

Social Problems. South Bend, Ind.: Society for the Study of
Social Problems, 1953-.

Sociological Quarterly. Columbia, Mo.: Sociological
Quarterly, 1960-.

Sociological Review. Staffordshire, England: University of
Keele, 1908-.

Sociology and Social Research: An International Journal.
Los Angeles: University of Southern California, 1916-.

Sociometry: A Journal of Research in Social Psychology.
Washington, D. C.: American Sociological Association,
1932-.

Chapter 9 - Evaluating Book-Length Studies

Book Review Digest. New York: Wilson, 1905-.

Book Review Index. Detroit: Gale Research Co., 1965-.

Chapter 10 - United States Government Publications

Wynkoop, Sally. Subject Guide to Government Reference Books. Littleton, Colo.: Libraries Unlimited, 1972.

Lu, Joseph. U. S. Government Publications Relating to the Social Sciences: A Selected Annotated Guide. Beverly Hills: Sage Publications, 1975.

Chapter 11 - United States Census Publications

U. S. Bureau of the Census. Census Bureau Programs and Publications: Area and Subject Guide. Washington, D. C.: Government Printing Office, 1968.

U. S. Bureau of the Census. Census of Population. Washington, D. C.: Government Printing Office, 1790-.

U. S. Bureau of the Census. Current Population Reports. Washington, D. C.: Government Printing Office, 1947-.

U. S. Bureau of the Census. Directory of Federal Statistics for Local Areas. Washington, D. C.: Government Printing Office, 1966.

U. S. Bureau of the Census. Directory of Federal Statistics for States. Washington, D. C.: Government Printing Office, 1967.

U. S. Bureau of the Census. 1970 Census User's Guide. Washington, D. C.: Bureau of the Census, 1970.